INVESTING
QuickStart Guide™

INVESTING

QuickStart Guide™

The Simplified Beginner's Guide to Successfully
Navigating the Stock Market, Growing Your Wealth,
& Creating a Secure Financial Future

Ted D. Snow, CFP®, MBA

ClydeBank
FINANCE

Editor: Marilyn Burkley
Cover Illustration and Design: Katie Poorman, Copyright © 2018 by ClydeBank Media LLC
Interior Design: Katie Poorman, Copyright © 2018 by ClydeBank Media LLC

ClydeBank Media LLC | PO Box 6561 Albany, NY 12206
Printed in the United States of America

Publisher's Cataloging-In-Publication Data
(Prepared by The Donohue Group, Inc.)

Names: Snow, Ted D.
Title: Investing quickstart guide : the simplified beginner's guide to successfully navigating the stock market, growing your wealth, & creating a secure financial future / Ted D. Snow, CFP, MBA.
Other Titles: Investing quick start guide
Description: [First edition]. | Albany, NY : ClydeBank Finance, [2018] | Includes bibliographical references and index.
Identifiers: ISBN 9781945051869 (paperback) | ISBN 9781945051326 (hardcover) | ISBN 9781945051951 (ebook)
Subjects: LCSH: Investments. | Stocks. | Finance, Personal.
Classification: LCC HG4521 .S66 2018 (print) | LCC HG4521 (ebook) | DDC 332.6--dc23

LCCN: 2017955870

ISNI: 0000 0004 6456 9247

Copyright © 2018
ClydeBank Media LLC
www.clydebankmedia.com
All Rights Reserved

ISBN-13 : 978-1-945051-86-9

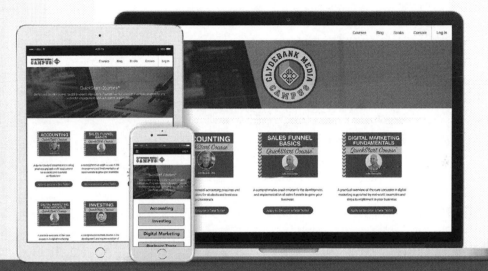
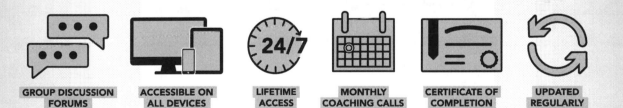

Contents

BEFORE YOU START READING, DOWNLOAD YOUR FREE DIGITAL ASSETS!

Visit the URL below to access your free Digital Asset files that are included with the purchase of this book.

☑ **Summaries**   ☑ **White Papers**
☑ **Cheat Sheets**   ☑ **Charts & Graphs**
☑ **Articles**   ☑ **Reference Materials**

DOWNLOAD YOURS HERE:

www.clydebankmedia.com/investing-assets

Introduction

You don't need to be a rocket scientist. Investing is not a game where the guy with the 160 IQ beats the guy with the 130 IQ.

— WARREN BUFFETT

We all understand investing essentials, right? Buy low, sell high, turn a profit. If you are reading this book, however, then odds are you are looking for a more detailed perspective. You want to learn how to make your money grow and work for you. You want to provide a good life for yourself and your family and to secure a worry-free retirement.

There is very little formal academic curriculum—even at the college level—devoted to training our youth on the importance of saving and investing. Financial education is too often a solitary pursuit, pitting the would-be learner (you) against a sparse and often confusing landscape full of investment "gurus," television personalities, and yes, unlicensed authors who want you to believe that if you would only subscribe to their programs, you would be well on your way to becoming the next Warren Buffett.

While researching this title, I found that a lot of do-it-yourself investment books are heavy on hype but lacking in substance. There are certainly some good ones out there, many of which we will reference and discuss within this book, but generally speaking it is hard to find good help these days, especially when it comes to beginner-friendly books. Many so-called beginner-friendly investment books appear to be written primarily to showcase the author's stock-picking subscription service and are lacking in any good faith attempt to lay out and explain the fundamentals of good investing practice. Other beginner-level titles speed through investing basics, choosing instead to focus on the author's complicated and often dubious "beat the market every time" stock market strategy.

Investing with Eyes Forward & Feet on the Ground

Good investing is not about what might have happened had you possessed the foresight to buy stock in Apple at twelve dollars a share back in 2008, or Wal-Mart when it first went public in the fall of 1970. Good investing actually has very little to do with one's ability to predict the future. Rather, it is about making simple, sound, and disciplined decisions right now, in the present. It is about making decisions in a way that lays the groundwork for wealth accumulation and a strong, secure financial future.

Make no mistake, had you purchased 100 shares in Wal-Mart in 1970 you would be rich, a multimillionaire. But to the average investor, sitting at his kitchen table in 1970, scanning the business section of his local newspaper in search of a good stock to buy, Wal-Mart doesn't look any more attractive than a tried and true railroad stock or perhaps that new paper mill company that just went public. We are always going to need paper, right?

In early 2009, before Apple set off on its upward trajectory that would culminate in its becoming the most highly valued company of all time, it was but one among several tech companies looking to make a big splash with mobile handheld devices. Research In Motion (RIM)—a Canadian company best known for making the Blackberry smartphone—was about 33 percent as valuable as Apple Inc. in 2009. In light of the fact that RIM was primarily selling handheld devices, not laptop or desktop computers, being 33 percent as valuable as one of the world's top computer companies was an impressive feat. Undoubtedly there was no shortage of investors eager to pour their capital into RIM in 2009, thinking that the sleek and business-savvy Blackberry, not the iPhone, would lead the way into the era of the smartphone. In 2017, RIM (now Blackberry Ltd.) is about half of 1 percent as valuable as Apple Inc.

When it comes to investing, time is the ultimate storyteller and the sole arbiter of success and failure. If you know what you are doing, then you can use this fact to your advantage. Evidence, much of which we will discuss at length in this book, shows that attempts at predicting market behavior are at best a waste of energy, and at worst disastrous for your portfolio.

If you are looking for the next big breakout investment or a list of hot stock tips, then I suggest you put down this book and turn to the top-ten pick lists, the bloggers, the brokers, and the TV personalities—the same people who told you to load up on RIM in 2009.

What I am going to teach you is an eyes-forward, feet-on-the-ground approach to investing, with an emphasis on long-term wealth-building strategy. I am not a speculator and I do not spend hours poring over stock charts trying to spot "trends." What I do is as simple as paying attention to the securities in which I invest. I buy when a security is being undervalued by the market, and I sell when it is overvalued. I seek out opportunities to diversify and maximize potential returns. I am a consummate investor, not a trader, and if you are not clear on the distinction you will be by the time you finish this book.

Though my personal investment philosophy is threaded throughout the text, you will find much of the content contained here more objective and encyclopedic in nature, complete with easy-to-reference chapter headings and a glossary of terms. You do not need to read this book straight through. Feel free to skip from chapter to chapter and from section to section as you see fit.

If you are brand new to investing, then I do recommend reading the book straight through, as we have done our best to introduce topics and vocabulary in a logical, sequenced manner that lends itself to easy learning. The goal of this text is, after all, to be the quintessential beginner's guide to investing. Nevertheless, given the range of topics analyzed and discussed, more experienced investors are sure to learn a thing or two as well.

While I am familiar with almost all types of investments, my personal expertise is in mutual funds, stocks, bonds, and ETFs, the kinds of securities that in my judgment are the most appropriate entry points for the beginner-level investor. Having launched and managed my own financial services company, I have had the privilege of helping countless individuals of varying backgrounds pursue and achieve their financial goals, and I hope that through this book I can do the same for you.

Though we will briefly touch on commodities, futures, REITs, options, penny stocks, and the Forex market, this book's primary focus will be on public stocks, bonds, mutual funds, and ETFs. We will not be covering private equity investing, angel investing, or self-managed real estate investments.

Stocks as the Currency of the Corporation

You know what a stock is, but I am wondering whether you think about stocks in the same way I do, particularly with regard to how they relate to US dollars (or your native country's currency). Stocks, like dollars, are an investment position. Technically speaking, *stocks* represent your share of ownership in a corporation, but let's abandon technicality for a moment. Instead, try thinking about stocks as a kind of corporate currency, one that, like US dollars, reflects the belief that its issuing entity, the company (or the government in the case of US dollars) will perpetuate itself and justify its value. This kind of mentality is helpful for new investors who are a little nervous about putting their money into the market. Think of the companies you are investing in as independent, trans-global entities—like countries, but for profit!

Take Exxon Mobil, for instance. Exxon Mobil's trading symbol (the string of letters used to identify a stock) is XOM. In January of 2018, XOM was trading on the ***New York Stock Exchange*** for a price of 86 dollars and 28 cents per share with a staggering market capitalization (combined worth of all outstanding shares of stock) of 351.35 billion dollars. If I decide to trade 8,628 of my US dollars to buy 100 shares of XOM, then I am doing little more than declaring my confidence that the institution of Exxon Mobil will perpetuate itself into the future and routinely deliver value back to the global marketplace. The value of my XOM shares will surely fluctuate but will *hopefully* appreciate in the long run—as the company improves and expands—and the XOM stock that I hold hopefully will appreciate at a rate that surpasses the appreciation potential of the US dollars I gave up in order to own XOM shares.

I could possibly lose all of my investment in the unlikely event that Exxon Mobil completely fails to justify its ongoing existence as a valid and solvent corporate entity. Similarly, had I chosen to keep my 8,628 US dollars rather than trade them for 100 shares of XOM, then I would still be subject to losing my money in the event that the US government failed to justify its ongoing existence as a valid and solvent government entity. Meanwhile, by betting my money on the US government rather than on Exxon Mobil, I would be investing in an entity obliged to priorities *other than* creating profit for myself and other investors. By contrast, one of the central missions of Exxon Mobil is to pursue profits for its investors. Therefore, if I have to put my faith (in the form of my money) somewhere, there is a good case to be made that my best option is to invest in an entity that is not only inclined to sustain itself but *also* inclined to pursue profit.

Companies issue stock after choosing to "go public." When going public, the owners of a company are essentially agreeing to dilute their personal equity in exchange for an influx of capital. *Equity* refers to a party's ownership percentage in a company. When a company first issues stock it is known as an ***initial public offering (IPO)***. A company that wants to go public will usually make a deal with an investment bank. The bank acts as an "underwriting firm," agreeing to temporarily buy up all shares of stock that the company intends to offer to the public. The underwriting firm is taking a risk by assuming it will be able to sell these shares to the public. Therefore, it charges the company a fee based on a certain percentage of the stock's agreed-upon price. An IPO is deemed successful if the underwriting firm meets the company's expectations by selling enough shares to the open market at a solid valuation. A good IPO may lead to a healthy "aftermarket" for the stock, where the stock will trade back and forth among a multitude of investors at a steadily appreciating price.

Stockholders own a share of ownership in the company proportionate to the number of shares they hold. Likewise, they own a proportionate share of the company's profits.

If Bryan owns 10 shares in company ABC, and company ABC has a total of 100 shares outstanding, then Bryan owns 10 percent of company ABC. If company ABC turns a profit of $100, then Bryan, theoretically, owns $10 of that profit.

fig. 1

ABC Company Shares

10% Owned by Bryan

Just because investors are theoretically entitled to their proportionate share of a company's profits does not mean that the company automatically starts cutting checks to investors as soon as a profit is realized. Some companies do not even pay their investors at all. They may use their profits instead for other purposes, such as paying down debt or expanding operations.

So, as an investor, why would you want to buy a company's stock if the company has no plans for sharing its profits with you? There are a couple of reasons. When a company turns consistent profits, gains significant market share, invents something wonderful or does anything else that drives up demand for its stock, the price of the stock goes up.

Janet buys 10 shares of XYZ stock for $10 per share, a total investment of $100. After Janet's stock purchase, XYZ turns a sizable profit for four consecutive quarters. The value of XYZ is now worth $13 per share. Janet's 10 shares are now worth $130.

When a stock owned by an investor rises in value, the investor becomes the beneficiary of either a realized or unrealized *capital gain*. The investor has the option of selling the stock for a profit, or she may choose to hold onto it in hopes that it will continue to appreciate. If the investor chooses the former option—selling the stock for a profit—then the capital gain becomes a *realized capital gain*. If she chooses to hold onto the stock, then she is said to have an *unrealized capital gain*.

Generally speaking, capital gains are not taxable until they become *realized* capital gains. More on investment-related taxes will be discussed in chapter 3.

In addition to capital gains, investors may benefit financially from the payment of dividends. **Dividends** are cash payments issued by the company to its investors (stockholders) on a regular basis, usually quarterly. The amount of an investor's dividend payment is proportionate to the amount of stock owned. Many investors instruct their stockbrokers to automatically reinvest their dividends. Other investors depend on the regular payment of stock dividends to support their day-to-day financial needs.

Not all companies that issue stock choose to issue dividends as well. For many investors, the promise of dividends makes a stock more attractive (dividends may also positively affect the stock's value), but there are plenty of stocks out there that perform well without issuing dividends. When stocks perform poorly, dividends will often decrease in value or be withheld altogether.

The Risks of *Not* Investing

Many would-be investors stay away from the stock market because they do not want to put their hard-earned money at risk. Risk is a very important factor that should be considered very seriously by investors. But the existence of risk is not in and of itself a good reason for keeping your cash hidden under your mattress when it could be working for you in the market.

The Inflation Risk

Idle cash is subject to inflation. If you leave large sums of money in a bank account for a long period of time, it may not be able to generate enough interest to outpace the rate of inflation. **Inflation** refers to the decline in purchasing power of a unit of currency, leading to higher and higher prices for the same goods. In the 1930s, for example, the cost of a new car was about $640. In the 1950s, buying a cup of coffee for five cents was to be expected. Generally speaking, a given basket of goods will continue to increase in price over time due to inflation.

From a government perspective, a moderate amount of inflation over time is a good thing. Higher prices for goods and services can result in higher profits for businesses, which allows for competitive wages and expanded productivity. Inflation also boosts the price of business assets, real estate, etc., which keeps overhead and other costs of production under control. If inflation sets in too rapidly, however—outpacing the ability of the economy to produce—then you have too many dollars chasing too few goods and services. Price inflation can lead to price distortion and dangerous economic misperceptions known as "bubbles." **Bubbles** refer to the severe overvaluation of a certain good, service, or commodity due to hype, rumor, or various other forms of herd behavior. Bubbles, by definition, are destined to pop, even if it takes months or years. When a bubble pops, actual economic value asserts itself over inflated economic value, and the inflated prices collapse suddenly, often causing economic turmoil.

Like stocks, rates of inflation can be highly volatile over time, and *deflation* may also set in, causing prices to decline. Unchecked deflation, just like unchecked inflation, can be damaging to the economy. When prices are too low, businesses have a harder time securing the profit margins they need to compensate their employees and expand their operations.

Due to monetary and fiscal policies—in addition to several other more abstract economic factors—inflation rather than deflation emerges as the most persistent phenomenon over time. Since 1913, the average annual rate of inflation has been 3.15 percent.[1] By contrast, savings accounts, even the most elite among them, offer a yield of about 1.5 percent in 2018.[2] In times like these, when interest rates are low, investing your money in stocks and other *securities* offers a potential buffer against the persistent inflationary tide.

Savings accounts offer higher yields during years when federal interest rates are higher. Currently, savings account yields do not keep up with inflation, but this is not to say that they never have in the past or will not in the future. An interest rate of 3.15 percent (the average rate of inflation) on a savings account is not unheard of.

Investing in the stock market provides a solution to the problem of lost cash value due to inflation. Even though the market is inherently volatile, stocks on average climb higher and higher in value over time. A look at the Dow Jones Industrial Average since 1910 reveals a pattern of persistent growth.

Not to say it is impossible to experience enormous, even devastating losses in the stock market, but the patient, experienced investor, holding a diverse portfolio of well-qualified holdings, will know how to remain calm in down markets and allow the market the time it needs to recover. Since its inception in the late eighteenth century, the New York Stock Exchange has had a 100 percent track record of recovery, even after substantial stock market downturns. A patient, straightforward, common-sense approach to investing will reward the long-term investor.

DOW JONES INDUSTRIAL AVERAGE
- SINCE 1910 -

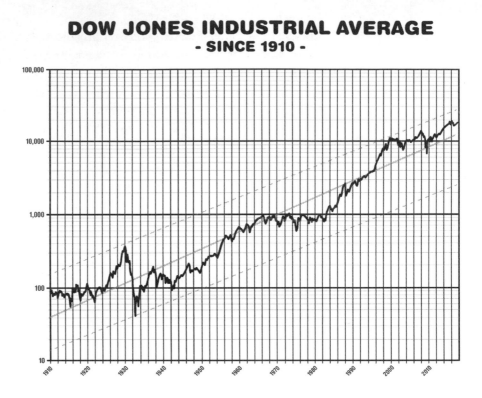

GRAPHIC

fig. 2

Lost Growth Opportunity

If we average out the performance of the stock market since it opened in the 1800s, we will observe a reliable annual return on investment equating to approximately 7 percent.[3] Nevertheless, many new investors view the stock market as more risky than it actually is. Driving this irrational fear is a very real phenomenon known as stock market volatility. In stock trader parlance, *volatility* refers to the degree to which a stock's price (or the price of a market as a whole) fluctuates. In October of 1929, the stock market suffered its greatest collapse in all of American history, losing about 20 percent of its total value over the course of a few days. Other major collapses in 1987, 2001/2002, and again in 2008/2009 crippled the net worth of countless investors, leaving a dramatic trust gap between Wall Street and Main Street. Nonetheless, in each of these major market collapses, the majority of investors who held their positions and waited for the market to recover were able to recoup their losses and then some. Faring even better were those investors who used the down market as an excuse to go on a buying spree, accumulating shares of several stocks on the cheap, many of which were due to rebound strongly over time.

Stock market calamities and tales of Wall Street greed make for powerful stories. They can dissuade people from investing in the market. The stories that do not get shared as often—unless you watch the business news channels or read books about investing like this one—are stories about the millions of regular investors who have used sound techniques, avoided panic, and allowed their portfolio to flourish. In the fall of 2014, closely following the release of some bad press, the price of Walgreens stock fell from about $73 to $58. It's funny, I don't even remember the news story. I just remember that the market reacted by selling off shares of Walgreens, lowering the demand for its stock and thereby lowering the price. Seeing no lasting threat to the fundamental value of Walgreens, I bought $12,000 worth of the company's stock (about 200 shares) at a price close to $59 per share. By August 2015, about a year later, I sold out of the position at $86 per share for a 54 percent gain (a profit of about $6,500). A 54 percent gain over a year's time is fairly decent to begin with, but the fact that I used Walgreens stock to get there made this return all the more satisfying. Usually, a 54 percent return in one year requires an investment play a bit more risky than buying stock in a well-known drugstore chain.

Being a competent investor means assessing the risks of investing alongside the risks of not investing. As I like to say, "Safe is not always safe."[4] Even if you choose to hold all of your assets in cash, you are still vulnerable to the persistent tide of inflation eating away at your net worth.

When assessing investment risk and reward, it is important to always think in terms of "opportunity costs." Had I kept my $12,000 under my mattress rather than taking action after observing Walgreens being undervalued and unfairly punished by the market, then the cost of my inaction would have been $6,500 in lost profit. An opportunity cost is the value of the action you forgo in order to complete another action. If you decide to keep your money in a savings account rather than investing it in a well-diversified portfolio of securities, then your potential opportunity cost is the loss of capital gains, dividends, and other earnings that could have been yours had you chosen to put your money to work for you in the market.

How This Book Is Organized

This book is intended to be a broad, beginner-level resource for investors. We will be discussing across-the-board investment basics—terminology, investment types, and the basic metrics and strategies used when evaluating investments. We will also review the principal resources available to investors in both the traditional and virtual spaces.

Though a thorough discussion of derivative investments, options, penny stocks, and similar investment vehicles will be offered in chapter 6, this book's principal objective is to assist individuals who seek to reliably profit from sound, stable, long-term investment practices. Throughout the book we will be focusing primarily on traditional, buy-and-hold style, long-term investing. For readers who desire a more thorough treatment of options or penny stock trading, please see ClydeBank Finance's corresponding titles.[5,6]

Chapter by Chapter

» "Chapter 1: The Language of Investing" contains essentially every-thing you need to get started in the stock and bond markets. Here you will learn about the most common mechanics of stock and bond trading, the buying and selling processes, and how to track and eval-uate your progress in the market.

» You cannot participate in the market without some form of broker-age service. "Chapter 2: From Brokerages to Robo-Advisors, How to Choose Your Investment Services" will offer a survey of the current financial services market. As an avid and enthusiastic provider of financial management services, I will give you my insider's take on the industry and how to go about finding services that match your needs.

» In "Chapter 3: How to Use Time to Your Advantage, Grow Your Wealth, and Fund the Perfect Retirement," we will begin our tour of the core elements of market strategy that I want you to take away from your reading. This chapter will focus primarily on *long positions* (investing with the expectation that a purchased security will gain in value over time).

» "Chapter 4: Decision Time—Deciding When, Where, and How To Invest," covers the various decision-making processes that go into the selection of a stock or other security.

» "Chapter 5: Investment Strategies" broadens the scope of portfolio management and discusses dollar cost averaging and other basic strategies investors use to manage risk and maximize returns.

» "Chapter 6: The Short Game—Speculating, Risk-Taking, and Embracing the Drama of the Market" will introduce investment instruments and strategies associated with more short-term and high-risk investments. The trading of options, penny stocks, and futures will be discussed, along with the basic mechanics of short selling and buying stocks on margin.

» "Chapter 7: Investment Psychology," will examine in depth the fallacies of "market timing" and other tempting but ultimately destructive investment behaviors. We will also talk about the unique advantages that disciplined investors have in the market.

» "Chapter 8: Beyond Profit—Promoting Ethics and Social Responsibility through Investing" delves into the phenomenon of *socially responsible investing*—investment approaches that screen out investments conflicting with one's moral beliefs while emphasizing civic, humanitarian, and environmental values in addition to profit.

» "Chapter 9: Investing Your Way to Financial Freedom" explores the techniques of the financially independent investors who have used the interest and dividends of their investments to retire early and to provide a decent (and often very modest) livelihood for themselves.

| 1 |
The Language of Investing

Chapter Overview
- » Understanding Stocks and Bonds
- » Types of Transactions
- » Market Indexes

Price is what you pay. Value is what you get.

– WARREN BUFFETT

Burton Malkiel, best known for his classic book *A Random Walk Down Wall Street,* claimed that there are only four relevant investment categories: cash, bonds, stocks, and real estate. Perhaps more important than what Malkiel includes is what he omits. Collectibles, for instance—baseball cards, antiques, and other memorabilia—he claims are fine to have on hand for nostalgic purposes, so long as you do not expect them to steadily appreciate or to generate dividend payments, interest payments, or other yields that can steadily add to your wealth. Malkiel is also not so keen on the whole gold craze, which he sees, like baseball cards, as nice to have around but unlikely to appreciate over the long haul and unable to reward its owner with dividends.

Malkiel's philosophy holds that an investment should actively generate value for its owner in the form of real capital. This standard would, at least, apply to the bonds, stocks, and real estate, but what about cash? As we discussed in this book's introduction, cash is rather stagnant, even when parked in a "high interest" savings account. Malkiel describes cash as a kind of critical placeholder, needed primarily for its liquidity, so investors can act swiftly when opportunity presents itself. Holding a significant portion of your wealth in cash also provides a kind of personal emergency management fund in the event life throws you a curveball.[7] Cash may also be a useful investment vehicle when saving for a particular significant purchase, like a vehicle or a down payment on a home. While it may be tempting to feed funds for an upcoming home purchase into the stock market in the hope that your portfolio will soar and you will suddenly be upgraded into a nicer neighborhood, such an approach is not wise investment strategy. The stock market, at a moment's notice, can go down and stay down for months or years at a time. If you are intent on buying a home in the next few years or so, you do not want to put yourself in a situation where there is pressure on you to liquidate your stocks at a loss, so you can spend less money than you saved on your new home. The purpose of holding cash is to provide reliable, short-term access to purchasing power. You will find much more success with stocks when you get in for the long haul.

A soon-to-be home buyer choosing to keep saved assets in cash rather than stocks is but one example of a very important principle in investing: investments should be tailored to event timelines. If you are investing for a retirement that is still a couple of decades away, then you may be willing to take on a more aggressive investment approach to maximize growth opportunities. If you are starting a savings account for your three-year-old's college education, then you will want to tailor your investment plan for a fifteen-year time horizon.

Even when you are investing with the longer term in mind, it is still enormously tempting to keep your eye glued to market news, constantly recalculating how rich (or poor) you are hour by hour, day by day. This destructive impulse is fed by the swarms of investment literature, websites, and TV personalities that are constantly offering investment "advice." If you learn anything from this book, learn that there is absolutely nothing wrong with a low-maintenance approach to investing, meaning you do not need to watch your portfolio like a hawk; you can usually get by just fine by checking in every few weeks or even every few months. In fact, in terms of real success in the marketplace, low-maintenance investing has a high likelihood of resulting in the highest returns. Fewer trades mean fewer commissions paid to brokers. Moreover, plenty of evidence has accumulated showing that investors who hold their positions in a well-thought-out investment plan—as opposed to those who trade frequently and sell off fast during signs of trouble—are rewarded with consistently better returns from the market.[8] A smooth, steady-handed approach will also give you a significant advantage over those who attempt to "time the market," a tempting but hapless strategy we will discuss in more detail in chapter 4.

We have already talked about one of Malkiel's four investment pillars, cash. In this chapter we will formally introduce you to two others: stocks and bonds. Understanding how these securities operate will be critical to your success as an emerging all-star investor.

Malkiel's fourth pillar, real estate investing, will be discussed in chapter 3.

Stocks & Bonds

True to Malkiel's criteria, both stocks and bonds are investments that (in theory) actively provide value to the investor. Stocks do so by paying dividends or by appreciating in value. Bonds pay out interest payments, which, unlike dividends, are constant with a set rate. Bonds, like stocks, can be sold and bought on the open market once issued, and the price of any given bond may be influenced by a variety of factors that we will discuss later in this chapter. The advantage of dividend payments over interest payments is that there is no limit to how much money a stockholder can collect from a dividend payment. With bonds, the investor's interest payments are fixed. By contrast, if a stock-issuing company performs well beyond expectation, then the amount of the dividend payment may also be higher than expected.

Common Stocks vs. Preferred Stocks

Throughout this book, when we refer to "stock" of any kind you may assume that we are referring to common stock. Preferred stock, like common stock, is available for purchase on the open market and is often listed alongside a company's common stock with a small "pf" next to the name. Preferred stock is bought and sold at a price that is independent of the common stock price. Preferred stockholders receive their dividend payments before common stockholders do, and these dividend payments are fairly stable. If the company is successful and the dividend payment of the common stock is increased, the preferred stock dividend will remain the same. If the company finds itself on hard times and needs to reduce or eliminate its dividend payments, it will do everything possible to restore dividends for the preferred stockholders first. The company will also repay preferred stockholders for any dividends withheld during bad business periods *before* it resumes payment of dividends to common stockholders (this is known as cumulative repayment and is the policy for most, but not all, preferred stock issues). In the event that a company fails completely, holders of preferred stocks will be paid out before common stockholders when the company liquidates.

If the company has issued bonds, then the bondholders will be paid first following a liquidation, then the preferred stockholders, and finally, the common stockholders.

Unlike common stockholders, preferred stockholders do not usually hold any voting rights in the stock-issuing company. Common stockholders are legally endowed with the right to vote on various issues affecting the company, such as policy directives or the selection of the board of directors. As a common stockholder you will receive ballots by mail or may cast your votes online. In general, one vote per share of stock owned is the norm, though many companies modify the way shareholder votes are cast and counted. For instance, sometimes common stock is issued as "class A" or "class B." Usually class A shares of common stock confer more powerful voting rights, and these shares are usually issued to senior management, C-level executives, and members of the board. On one hand, the subdivision of common stock into classes can be problematic because it has the potential to give shareholders with less equity more power than shareholders with more equity. On the other hand, the subdivision of common stock insulates the company from takeover by outsiders with a lot of purchasing power.

ON COMMON STOCK VS. PREFERRED STOCK: My opinion is that if you are in the market for a preferred stock, then you are looking for a higher level of dividend income and a more stable share price. With common stock your focus will be more on price appreciation.

Bonds

Bonds are a form of debt whereby a government, a governmental department, a company, or some other entity seeks an immediate influx of cash while promising to pay interest for the duration of the bond and return the principal after the expiration of a fixed term. The US Treasury issues securities that are available for purchase with 1-month, 3-month, 6-month, 1-year, 2-year, 3-year, 5-year, 7-year, 10-year, and 30-year terms. A *term* refers to the period of time an investor must wait before the bond "matures" and the face value of the bond is returned to him. In the meantime, the bond generates a fixed income for the investor in the form of interest payments. While holding a bond, investors are paid, usually semiannually, at a rate that was agreed to at the time of the bond's purchase. Since bonds with longer terms (like 30-year bonds) require investors to part with their cash for longer periods of time, the interest rates are typically higher.

Talk the Talk

Term of the Treasury Security	Referred to as,
1 year or less	Treasury bill or T-bill
2 – 10 years	Treasury note or T-note
> 10 years	Treasury bond or T-bond

GRAPHIC

fig. 3

Treasury securities are either "bonds," "bills," or "notes"

They are issued for 1, 3, or 6 month terms and 1, 2, 3, 5, 10, 20, or 30 year terms

Collectively, Treasury securities are often referred to simply as "Treasuries"

Figure 4 shows the interest yield on treasury securities in early 2017. As you can see, the interest rate climbs higher as the security's term lengthens. This is known as a *normal yield curve.*

Interest Rates on Treasury Securities
A normal yield curve

GRAPHIC

fig. 4

Term of the Treasury Security	Interest
3-month	.50%
6-month	.62%
1-year	.80%
5-year	1.96%
10-year	2.47%

In the rare event that treasury securities with shorter terms are being sold with interest rates *higher* than securities with longer terms, watch out. This is known as an inverted yield curve and is seen as an indicator of an oncoming recession. Why might that be?

Think about the bond market as being in perpetual competition with the stock market for investor capital. The downside of buying US Treasury securities is that the potential return on average is going to be lower than that of the stock market. The upside is that the money invested is thought to be highly secure, exposed to a very limited amount of risk. The interest rates of US Treasury securities are indicators of general confidence in the economy. If investors are wary of putting their money in the stock market, then they are more willing to commit their cash to treasury bills, notes, and bonds, where they can enjoy a nearly guaranteed rate of return. If investors are optimistic about the stock market, then they are less inclined to invest in treasuries. They would rather put their money in stocks and get that 7 or 8 percent (or better!) return. In the latter scenario (where the stock market looks attractive) the demand for treasury bills goes down, and in order to compete with other investment opportunities, the government is forced to issue treasuries at higher interest rates. When the stock market does not look so appetizing, then demand rises for treasuries, and the government can auction them off at lower interest rates. In this way, the interest rates on treasury securities (the 10-year note in particular) are often regarded as a type of barometer for investor confidence in the stock market.

Treasury securities of varying terms are issued at auction by the US Treasury several times a year, though they may also be purchased in the secondary market (after they have been issued).

Returning to our question regarding the inverted yield curve as a sign of pending market recession: If the interest rate on the 3-month treasury bill is suddenly higher than that of the 1-year treasury bill, then it is a signal that investors feel trouble is ahead and that, maybe not in three months' time, but in a year's time, the economy may become stagnant or it may recede, which would likely drive up demand for treasury securities. Therefore, holding a 1-year bill at an abnormally low interest rate may very well be the right play, as demand for that bill will rise when the stock market sours.

Since World War II, every time an inverted yield curve has asserted itself it has been followed by either a significant economic downturn or a full-blown recession within a year to eighteen months. Watching the yield curve on treasuries is an interesting exercise in gleaning economic sentiment among investors. During the 2016 election season, for instance,

Hillary Clinton's apparent likely victory seemed to correlate with a flattening of the yield curve. Investors flocked to longer-term treasury notes and bonds, bidding down the interest rates offered by these securities. The unexpected election of Donald Trump, with his promises of reduced regulations and tax cuts, increased investor demand for stocks (thereby lowering demand for longer-term treasuries), causing higher stock prices and higher interest rates on longer-term treasuries. When investors are bullish about the market, they are less interested in tying up their capital in treasuries. In the face of reduced demand, treasuries must offer higher interest rates in order to attract capital.

When it comes to using treasuries to evaluate investor confidence, longer-term treasuries offer more information than shorter-term treasuries. Shorter-term treasuries (bills) are heavily influenced by something known as the "federal funds rate." The federal funds rate is the interest rate at which banks may lend to one another overnight and without any collateral. When the federal funds rate is high, capital becomes more expensive, which slows down economic growth. When the federal funds rate is low, capital is more easily obtained, and it is therefore easier for businesses to attempt expansions and for new businesses to get started. The idea is to promote steady and sustainable economic growth. Grow too fast and the economy will end up in bubble territory, while overly slow or stagnant growth can lead to fewer jobs and lower wages. The federal funds rate is established, reviewed, and revised by a committee called the Federal Open Market Committee, a part of the Federal Reserve.

Treasury securities as well as other types of bonds can be resold after they have been purchased and before they mature. In fact, very few bonds are bought by investors at auction and then held onto by the same investor until maturity. They are normally resold several times over in what are called "secondary markets." Bond trading on the secondary market is usually facilitated in the same way that stock trading is facilitated—by brokers. The current price of bonds is affected by the interest rates of similar bonds currently being issued. Treasuries with higher interest rates (relative to the treasuries currently being issued) will command higher prices in the secondary market, and treasuries with lower rates will sell at lower prices.

EXAMPLE

Let's say that I buy a 10-year treasury note today, directly from the government, for a price of $1,000 (treasuries are sold in increments of $1,000 when issued by the government, though they can be sold at any price on the secondary market).

Per Figure 4, holding this note means that the treasury will pay me about $25 (2.47 percent of the note's face value) every six months in interest payments and will then, at the end of the ten-year term, pay me back the full $1,000 principal.

Now, let's say that I hold onto the note for a year and the stock market takes a turn for the worst. There is suddenly much greater demand for treasury securities, and they are being auctioned off with interest rates much lower than 2.47 percent.

The note that I bought last year now represents a much better investment than those available in the current bond market. Therefore, I will likely be able to sell my note for a price greater than $1,000. Neither the interest yield nor the face value of the note will change after I sell it to another party; it will still pay 2.47 percent semiannually and $1,000 at maturation. The market value of my T-note, however, may change at any time.

The reason the other party was willing to pay me more than $1,000 for the note was because their alternative was to purchase a new treasury security at auction with a lower interest rate. If the buyer is intent on putting her money in bonds (as many investors do in a down economy) then she may fare much better by buying my higher yield note at a higher price rather than buying a new lower yield note at face value. Meanwhile, I make a tidy profit.

All treasury securities do carry a degree of risk and the potential for high opportunity cost. If interest on treasury securities increases significantly after your purchase, then your bill, note, or bond will be worth less than what you paid for it in the aftermarket. You will either have to sell your security at a loss, or hold onto it and accept a rate of return that is not competitive relative to the current economy. The investor's opportunity cost in this scenario is represented in all of the other, better-performing investments he might have made had his money not been tied up in treasury securities.

Bonds are distinct from stocks in that they are a form of debt rather than equity. The US government cannot issue stock because it does not have any equity to sell. When you hold a bond you are acting as a creditor, not as an owner. In addition to the federal government, many other entities issue bonds in order to raise capital or pay down debt, including municipalities, states, and corporations. The interest paid on bonds is, in most

Moody's		S&P		Fitch		
Long Term	Short Term	Long Term	Short Term	Long Term	Short Term	
Aaa		AAA		AAA		Prime
Aa1		AA+	A-1+	AA+	A1+	High Grade
Aa2	P-1	AA		AA		
Aa3		AA-		AA-		
A1		A+	A-1	A+	A1	Upper Medium Grade
A2		A		A		
A3	P-2	A-	A-2	A-	A2	
Baa1		BBB+		BBB+		Lower Medium Grade
Baa2	P-3	BBB	A-3	BBB	A3	
Baa3		BBB-		BBB-		
Ba1		BB+	B	BB+	B	Non Investment Grade Speculative
Ba2		BB		BB		
Ba3		BB-		BB-		
B1		B+		B+		Highly Speculative
B2		B		B		
B3	Not Prime	B-		B-		
Caa		CCC+	C		C	Substantial Risks
Ca		CCC		CCC		Extremely Speculative
C		CCC-				In Default (with little prospect for recovery)
/				DDD		In Default
/		D	/	DD	/	
/				D		

GRAPHIC

fig. 5

instances, directly proportionate to the risk of default. Figure 5 depicts the rating scales for short- and long-term bonds as defined by the three most prominent credit rating agencies (Moody's, S&P, and Fitch).

Bonds with longer terms to maturity will usually pay more interest than shorter-term bonds (i.e., a ten-year treasury note will almost always pay more interest than a 1-year treasury bill). Also, the bonds with higher credit ratings (AAA, AA, etc.) generally offer lower interest yields, while the bonds with the lower ratings (BBB) offer the higher yields. As with nearly every investment opportunity, more risk means more potential reward.

Stocks vs. Bonds

While bonds certainly have their place in a well-balanced investment portfolio, particularly in those where stable and steady returns are required, they historically underperform stocks in terms of total return value. A study conducted by Kenneth French and his Nobel-prize-winning associate, Eugene Fama, found that stocks outperform bonds during any given 1-year, 5-year, 10-year, or 15-year period.[9]

Stocks vs. T-Bills According to Fama/French

GRAPHIC

fig. 6

Evaluation Period	Stocks Outperform Treasuries
1 year	69% of the time
5 year	78% of the time
10 year	85% of the time
15 year	96% of the time

Reading Stock Tickers & Stock Tables

When I was coming up in the financial services industry in the late '80s, we did not have stock tracking apps or smartphones, but we were nevertheless perfectly inundated with up-to-the-second market updates. There were screens everywhere, big electronic tickers above the receptionist's desk, computers—wherever we were on the floor, we were sure to be in eyeshot of the latest info from the market. Were we to go back even further in time to the 1950s and 1960s, we would find market news being punched out by a telegraph-like machine onto a thin paper ribbon, a piece of paper about three times the width of what you would find inside a fortune cookie. Such were the trappings of the industry professionals. The layman investor, for many generations, would get his market news from the business section of the local newspaper.

While stock tables are still regularly published in print, more and more investors have turned to websites and customizable electronic applications. From Times Square to your iPhone, stock tickers can be found in a multitude of places and in a variety of different formats. Figure 7 is an example of a standard stock ticker.

GRAPHIC

fig. 7

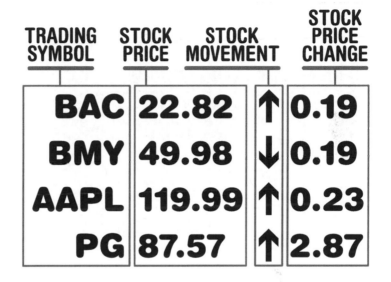

TRADING SYMBOL	STOCK PRICE	STOCK MOVEMENT	STOCK PRICE CHANGE
BAC	22.82	↑	0.19
BMY	49.98	↓	0.19
AAPL	119.99	↑	0.23
PG	87.57	↑	2.87

Each stock is referred to by a unique series of one to five letters. These unique signatures are known as trading symbols. Trading symbols are often derived from company initials or abbreviations of the company name. BAC, for instance, are the initials of Bank of America Corporation, and AAPL is an abbreviation for Apple Inc. Stocks that appear on the New York Stock Exchange (NYSE) usually have one (F, Ford Motor Company), two (PG, Procter & Gamble), or three letters (BMY, Bristol-Myers Squibb Co.). More recently, about a hundred NYSE stocks have been allowed to use four-letter symbols (like YUMC, Yum China Holdings Inc., and BABA, Alibaba Group Holding Ltd.). Stocks that appear on the Nasdaq exchange usually have four (NAVI, Navient Corporation) or five letters (NRCIA, National Research Corporation).

Some companies use a creative trading symbol that does not reflect the company's name but instead reflects its industry, signature product, or history. Anheuser-Busch InBev, for instance, trades under the symbol BUD, and Aqua America Inc. trades under the symbol WTR.

In the ticker in Figure 7, the stock's current price (in dollars) is listed immediately to the right of its trading symbol, followed by a description of the stock's movement for the day. BAC, as Figure 7 shows, is up 19 cents for the day.

In addition to the change in price, many stock tickers will also show the percentage change in overall value for a stock. Market indexes, like the Dow Jones Industrial Average and the S&P 500, also show up on stock tickers, as do many exchange traded funds. (Market indexes are discussed in greater detail later in this chapter, and exchange traded funds (ETFs) are discussed in chapter 3.)

fig. 8

YTD % CHG	52 Wk HIGH	52 Wk LOW	Stock	Trading Symbol	Div	Yield %	P/E	Volume	Close	Net CHG
27.9	74.99	38.71	Ferrari N.V.	RACE	.67	0.99	29.89	618,324	67.30	-0.05
95.3	2.23	.87	Pac Coast Oil Trust	ROYT	.03	9.45	353.12	150,910	2.09	1.01
13.7	10.56	8.12	PIMCO Strategic Income Fund	RCS	.07	8.72	-	141,070	9.91	0.14
-24.1	32.83	11.03	R.R. Donnelley & Sons Co	RRD	.14	4.52	-	1.63 M	12.40	0.16
4.7	19.87	9.29	Radiant Group Inc	RDN	.00	0.05	13.96	1.48 M	18.82	0.10
55.9	6.29	2.45	Radiant Logistics Inc	RLGT	-	-	570.36	406,681	6.08	-0.14
-11.8	114.00	75.62	Ralph Lauren Corp	RL	.50	2.48	46.17	1.13 M	80.57	0.96
-19.8	46.96	26.24	Range Resources Corp	RRC	.02	0.29	-	4.80 M	27.56	0.33
8.5	81.92	75.09	Raymond James Financial, Inc	RJF	.22	1.17	19.12	1.71 M	75.19	0.11
-15.6	17.39	9.59	Rayonier Advanced Materials	RYAM	.07	2.15	8.73	398,297	13.05	-0.09
9.9	157.59	124.98	Raytheon Company	RTN	.80	2.04	20.98	1.49 M	156.01	-0.02

Source: Data from Google Finance - Google and the Google logo are registered trademarks of Google Inc., used with permission.

Stock tables will generally offer more extensive details about stocks, such as dividend yield and price-earnings ratio (P/E ratio). Figure 8 is an example of a standard stock table that can be found in the business section of major newspapers.

In the following section, we will explore some key stock metrics, including those featured in Figure 8.

Essential Stock Metrics & Data Points

Price

A stock's price is the cost in dollars required to purchase one share of the company. While a stock's price is its most visible and talked-about descriptor, absent any contextualizing information it is quite an arbitrary metric, telling us very little. To get a clearer idea of how a stock's price relates to its value, a multitude of factors must be taken into consideration alongside the price. For example, if we take the number of shares of the stock that are outstanding and multiply this number by the stock's price, then we arrive at the market capitalization for the stock, which is a more informative metric.

Market Capitalization

Market capitalization reflects the total market value of a company. This metric is generally used by investors to gain a sense of how large or small a company is. Market capitalization, not stock price, is what truly speaks to how the market views the scale of a company's operations.

Returning to Figure 8, let's take a look at Ferrari N.V. (RACE). Even though market capitalization is not listed in the stock table, we can easily calculate it by looking up the number of outstanding shares. For the record, "volume" (shown in Figure 8) and "total outstanding shares" (not shown in Figure 8) are not the same thing.

Let's say that we jump on Google or Yahoo! Finance and find out that RACE currently has 188.9 million shares outstanding. By multiplying this number by RACE's stock price, 67.30, we arrive at a market capitalization of about 12.7 billion.

Figure 8 lists the stock's price under the column labeled "close," referring to the stock's price at the close of the market the previous trading day.

Though it is good to know what market capitalization is and how it is calculated, you will not have much trouble finding market cap data for stocks listed on your brokerage's website or on other internet-based financial data services like Google or Yahoo! Finance.

Currently, and for the last several years, the publicly traded company with the largest market cap is Apple Inc. at 617 billion, making it the most valuable company ever to exist.

Stocks are often discussed in terms of their market capitalization values. "Large-cap" refers to stocks with high market capitalization. Ten billion or above is generally considered large-cap, though as we can see with Apple, there is still plenty of room to grow after hitting the ten-billion mark. Mid-cap stocks generally fall somewhere in the two-billion to ten-billion market cap range, and small-cap stocks can be under two billion but should be at least three hundred million. In Wall Street parlance, stocks with market caps between fifty and three hundred million are known as "micro-caps" and stocks with market caps less than fifty million are known as "nano-caps."

In chapter 6, we will discuss penny stocks. A penny stock is defined by the SEC (Securities and Exchange Commission) as any stock that trades below five dollars per share. Other definitions hold that a stock must trade at below one dollar per share in order to be considered a penny stock.

Trading Volume

Trading volume is a measure of the quantity of shares traded during a given period. In Figure 8 we can see that RACE was trading at a volume of 618,324.

Why is volume important, or even relevant? There are many reasons, but let's look at two of the biggest ones. First, a stock's trading volume adds credibility to a developing trend. If a stock declines in value over the course of a week and the trading volume is exceptionally high, then you can conclude that a lot of buyers and sellers believe that the stock is lowering in value and that the trend is strong and will likely continue. If the stock's price is climbing in conjunction with a spike in trading volume, then there is reason to believe that the trend has momentum. On the flip-side, if a stock price fluctuates while trading volume is low, then it is more likely to be the result of a few erratic or random trades, and the apparent trend should not be given as much credence.

Trading volume can also be used to assess the liquidity and marketability of a stock. *Liquidity* is a measure of how fast a stock can be turned into cash, and marketability refers to the extent to which a market exists for the stock. The two terms are similar, almost meaning the same thing. Usually, a stock that is highly marketable will also be highly liquid.

A rare case of high liquidity alongside low marketability might involve a company, ABC, that has issued stock that very few investors want to buy. Despite its fledgling stock, the company is sitting on an excess of capital and decides to buy back shares of its own stock, ensuring liquidity for its current investors.

A more technical definition of **marketability** is the ability to trade an asset at a given price at a given volume. Under this definition, marketability becomes more of a relative term, best considered in the context of a particular investment predicament. A large institutional investor that needs to purchase several million shares in a stock and wants to do so at $20 per share may find the marketability of a stock problematic, whereas a casual investor looking to purchase ten shares of the same stock at a flexible price point may find no marketability problem whatsoever.

Smaller companies generally have a smaller pool of investors. Therefore, trading volume, liquidity, and marketability are especially relevant concerns when trading in small-cap stocks, funds comprised of small-cap stocks, and penny stocks. In order to sell a stock and realize a profit, you have to have a buyer. Usually it is not too difficult to find a buyer for a major, well-known stock, but in the less populated marketplaces, like the penny stock exchanges, traders routinely find themselves wanting to sell (or buy) but without anyone to do business with. In this sense, the higher the stock's trading volume, the higher its liquidity and marketability, and the easier it will be to buy and sell the stock when the time comes.

Because of the significance of trading volume, many investors utilize price-to-volume charts, which concurrently track fluctuations in a stock's price with fluctuations in its trading volume. See Figure 9.

fig. 9

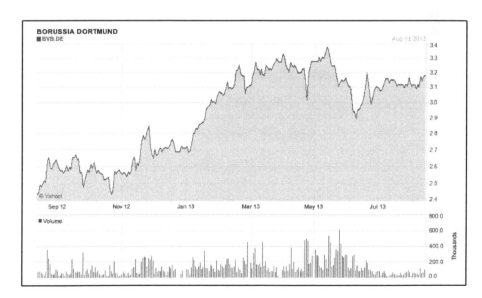

The price-to-volume chart above tracks the price and trading volume of a penny stock called Borussia Dortmund, a publicly traded German football club.

P/E (Price-Earnings) Ratio

In Figure 8, you will notice a column labeled P/E. This stands for *price-earnings ratio* and is one of the most commonly discussed and evaluated metrics relied upon by traders, especially when considering whether a stock is "cheap" or "expensive."

fig. 10

$$P/E = \frac{\text{The Stock Price per Share}}{\text{Annual Earnings per Share}}$$

P/E is calculated by dividing the price of a stock by its earnings per share (EPS). A good way to illustrate the importance of this metric is by scaling it down to the level of a small business. Let's say there is an auto mechanic who runs a parts and repair shop and the shop has brought in a million dollars in earnings over the last four quarters. The owner of the shop decides that he wants to sell the shop and is asking twenty million dollars. The price-earnings ratio of the auto shop is thus 20:1, or 20. At a glance, it may appear that this is a fairly expensive proposition. If you bought the auto shop, then you would theoretically have to wait twenty years before realizing a full return on your investment. But such a view only takes into account earnings, not capital gains. If the business improves over time, then you have the potential not only to boost earnings higher than $1M, but you can also resell the business at a higher price (which is much easier to do after earnings go up).

Now, let's say that you are seriously interested in buying the auto shop for twenty million. You are about ready to pull the trigger on the deal when a friend of yours tells you that there is another auto shop that just went on the market. This auto shop brought in 1.5 million over the last four quarters and the owner is asking twenty-eight million for the business.

Based solely on price-earnings, which auto shop is the better buy?

Answer: The P/E for the first auto shop is 20. The P/E for the second shop is 28:1.5, or 18.67. Looking only at P/E, the second shop is a better deal.

To calculate the *earnings per share* of a stock, divide the company's total earnings in dollars by the number of total shares outstanding. P/E allows investors to give more meaning to the otherwise arbitrary price of a stock.

Stocks with a high P/E are considered expensive; more dollars have to be spent for each dollar of earnings. Low P/E stocks are considered "cheap," in a good way. The P/E metric is not only used to evaluate stocks but can also be calculated and evaluated with respect to entire indexes, funds, and even personal portfolios.

Some stocks will not have their P/E listed. This is either because there is no current data available to calculate P/E, or because the P/E is actually negative, because the company has been losing money.

"Annual earnings" are the net earnings accrued over the previous four quarters.

Usually, the P/E you find listed in a stock table is the "trailing" P/E, meaning that it reflects the stock's earnings over the last four quarters. A "forward" P/E is another way of assessing P/E, whereby analysts combine the data from the last two quarters with their projections for the next two quarters. Obviously, forward P/E will not always be as accurate as trailing P/E, but it could prove useful. For instance, if new market forces appear or big news comes out that is relevant to the welfare of the company, a forward PE will be able to take this new information into account.

The Difference Between "Earnings" & "Profit"

Earnings, not profit, are used to calculate a stock's P/E ratio. Earnings and profit are similar but certainly not identical concepts. Earnings refer to the amount of money taken in minus the costs of the goods sold and minus the costs of all other efforts that immediately contributed to the revenue gain. Profit is wider in scope, including an account of all other overhead and administrative costs. Over any given period, a company's profit will be less than its earnings. In small business terms, "earnings" are the equivalent of gross profit, and "profit" is the equivalent of net profit.

Dividend Yield

Returning to Figure 8, there are two columns in the stock table that provide information about dividends: the DIV column and the YLD % column. The DIV column quotes the current annual dividend of the stock. RACE is quoted at .67, meaning that for each share of Ferrari N.V. stock owned, an investor would be paid 67 cents in dividends over the course of a year. The YLD % column shows the current dividend as a percentage of the stock's overall price. Investors who rely on their stock portfolios to provide a stream of steady income are more inclined to be concerned with DIV and YLD %. Investors also compare YLD % to interest yields offered by bonds. Dividends are usually issued in quarterly payments. If there is nothing listed in the DIV and YLD % columns, then the stock does not pay a dividend.

Volatility

Stock tables and listings will usually provide investors with a way of evaluating a stock's price volatility. Volatility refers to the extent to which a stock is inclined to fluctuate in price. Investors who purchase high volatility stocks should brace themselves for a wild ride.

In our Figure 8 stock table, the columns that speak to the volatility of a stock are the YTD % CHG column and the 52-week Hi/Lo columns. The YTD % CHG stands for year-to-date percent change. It is a measure of how much the stock has changed since the first day of the calendar year. The 52-week Hi/Lo columns display the highest and lowest prices at which the stock has traded throughout the previous 52 weeks. Stocks that issue dividends tend to exhibit less volatility than stocks that do not.

Volatility is of particular relevance for options traders (see chapter 5). When certain options strategies are employed, any degree of significant volatility (up or down) during a given time period will result in a profit.

Buying & Selling Stocks

Buying and selling stocks (also known as trading) is how you make money in the stock market. As you probably already know, you buy a stock when you think its value is likely to increase, and you sell when you think the value is likely to go down. In order to buy and sell stock, you need to open an account with a stockbroker or a brokerage firm. These regulated professional entities are authorized to make transactions on stock exchanges on behalf of institutional and retail clientele. Accounts opened with brokers or brokerage firms are known simply as "brokerage accounts."

When making transactions through a brokerage account, it is helpful to think of all buying and selling as "trades," even if you are simply trading cash for stocks or vice versa. Brokers usually charge a commission or "ticket charge" on each trade you make. In a standard, do-it-yourself brokerage account—where investors do their own research and choose their own investments—this charge will usually be referred to as a "commission." If your assets are under management by a financial professional, then the charge will be referenced in your billings as a "ticket charge."

If you enlist the services of a financial professional, then you will usually also pay an annual fee based on the total value of the assets you have under management. However, the transaction commissions ("ticket charges") may be lower than what you would pay going it alone.

Some brokers offer customers a fixed number of discounted or free trades, either as a promotion for new customers or as a reward for legacy or high volume traders.

After you complete a trade, your broker is required to provide you with a written record of the transaction. Figure 11 is an example of a transaction record. Details include the number of shares bought or sold, the price of the purchase or sale, and the date on which the transaction took place.

fig. 11

ABC
BROKERAGE

ACCOUNT #: 87654321
TRADE DATE: 3/3/17
SETTLEMENT DATE: 3/8/17

YOU BOUGHT: MINING CORP. (MNGC)

TRADE NUMBER	QUANTITY	PRICE	PRINCIPAL	COMMISSION	FEES	NET AMOUNT
32165487	10.00000	$50.50000	$505.00	$5.00	$3.00	$513.00

In figure 11, the "quantity" column lists the number of stock shares purchased (or sold). The "price" column shows the per-share purchase price (or selling price) of the stock. Multiplying quantity by price gives us the "principal," the total amount of money being invested in the stock for this purchase. If you are selling a stock, then the principal will indicate the total amount of money being received for the sale of the stock before commissions and fees are deducted. In order to arrive at the true cost of the trade, you must account for the expenses of the purchase (commissions, fees, etc.). In Figure 11, this added expense is reflected in the "net amount."

In the upper right-hand corner of Figure 11, you will see the **settlement date**. This refers to the date at which the transfer of money for stock (or vice versa) actually took place. If the transaction date is the date on which the deal is agreed to, then the settlement date is the date on which the goods are actually delivered and payment is made. The settlement date is particularly relevant to investors who are liquidating stock or other securities so that they can spend the cash. If you are trying to buy a car or a home, or go on vacation, then you want to know when you will have the cash on hand from your sale.

For a long time, settlement dates occurred three business days after the transaction date—"t + 3" in investment parlance. As of September 5, 2017, at the behest of a lot of industry lobbying, the SEC has moved that day up by one to "t + 2," meaning that the settlement date now occurs within two business days following the transaction date.[10]

If your plan is to sell one stock (or other security) and buy another stock right away, then you will not have to wait for the first transaction to settle before initiating your next transaction (the buy). You can order the sell and the buy on the same day, because the settlement date for both orders will be the same.

Bob has a brokerage account worth $500, all of it invested in stock XYZ. He wants to sell all of his XYZ stock and buy $500 worth of ABC stock. If he executes a sell order for XYZ on Monday, May 1st, then the transaction will probably settle by Thursday, May 4th. Bob's buy order for ABC can also be transacted on May 1st; this order will also likely settle on May 4th. The cash from the sale of XYZ will be in his account on May 4th, and therefore he will have the cash needed to settle his obligations as a buyer of ABC on the same date. Bottom line, you do not have to wait until your sale settles before using the proceeds to buy new stocks (or other securities).

This preceding example assumes that the stock is sold via a standard "market order." If the sale is initiated via a "limit order," then the investor's ability to immediately initiate a new buy order may be delayed. Market and limit orders are discussed in detail later in this chapter.

Stocks are bought and sold with the help of "**market makers**." These are firms that offer pricing quotes to the public while standing ready to buy and sell blocks of stock in accordance with prices they establish. Market makers give the stock market liquidity. Well-known stocks in well-known exchanges usually have several market makers, ten on average, though some have as many as fifty or more. Lesser-known stocks, trading on lesser-known markets (like the OTC Pink Sheets), do not have as many market makers, as the demand for these stocks is not nearly as constant. This is in part why penny stocks carry more risk; the lack of competition makes it easier for an investor to come across a penny stock that is priced well outside of its proper market value. In contrast, when you are dealing with stocks that are trading with heavy volume, you can at least have faith that the prices reflect a relatively accurate market value for the day.

Bid & Ask Prices

Market makers will quote both a *bid price* and an *ask price* for stocks (and other securities). The bid price quote tells us that there are buyers willing to purchase the stock, right now, at the stated bid price. The ask price quote tells us that there are sellers willing to sell the stock, right now, at the stated ask price. Figure 12 depicts a random sample stock listing offered by a typical market maker.

fig. 12

$82.41	-$0.13 ↓ -0.16% ↓		
Bid	$82.37	Size	40x1
Ask	$82.42	Volume	24,809,690

The $82.41 is the price you would typically see on a stock ticker. Though this price is a good indication of the current value of the stock, it is not actually a guarantee of the actual buying or selling price; $82.41 is the price reflecting the stock's most recent trading price. There is no guarantee that this price will still be available to the next investor who wants to buy or sell. Nevertheless, there is a reasonable expectation that the stock can be bought or sold at a price very close to its last known trading price. In Figure 12, the current bid price for the stock is $82.37. Buyers are bidding to purchase this stock, right now, for that price. Sellers are ready to sell, right now, for $82.42. As we can see, the most recent actual transaction took place at a price point just under the current ask price and a few cents over the current bid price.

Many market makers will also provide "size" information, describing the quantity of bids versus the quantity of asks that are active in the market. In Figure 12, the size is 40 x 1. For stocks that trade at high volumes, "size" is often listed in hundreds, so 40 x 1 would equate to 4,000 x 100. This means that there are 4,000 bids available at the listed bid price and 100 asks at the listed ask price. For a seller looking to unload 4,000 or fewer shares, the size information guarantees that this can be done at a price of $82.37 per share, whereas a prospective buyer can acquire up to 100 shares at a price of $82.42 per share. The higher demand coming from this stock's potential buyers may also explain why the stock's last sale price of $82.41 is closer to the ask price than to the bid price.

Now that you understand the meaning of bid and ask prices, you are ready to actually buy and sell. There are a few different ways to do this.

Market & Limit Orders

When you put in a market order to buy or sell a stock, your brokerage will generally guarantee that the transaction will go through right away. A *market order* finds the best immediate market price for your transaction. When selling, if the stock is being traded in high volumes and the bid size is substantial, then you will usually be able to get the current bid price for your stock, though this is generally not guaranteed by your brokerage. Depending on how fast the trade is executed and how volatile the stock, a market order may result in a transaction falling outside the bid-to-ask spread, meaning that sellers may have to settle for a price below the bid price and buyers may have to pay more than the ask price.

Nevertheless, market orders are a convenient and expedient way of solidifying or liquidating your position in a stock security. For traders focused on long-term positions and who are comfortable buying or selling close to the last transaction price (the main price listed on the stock ticker), market orders are an efficient and sensible way to trade. Also, if you are anticipating a big move in a stock over the next few days or weeks and want to buy in or sell out fast, market orders are the way to go.

Limit orders are used when the investor is keen on setting his own price. Unlike with a market order, there is no guarantee that the transaction will go through right away or at all. Many brokers and brokerage firms allow investors to specify a time frame for their limit orders. Most brokerages will allow you to specify your limit price and then specify a duration. You can either instruct the brokerage to cancel the order if the transaction at the limit price is not achieved before the end of the trading day or you can instruct the broker to search for the limit price for a sixty-day period. At any time during the sixty-day period, assuming the transaction has yet to be filled, you as the investor may cancel the limit order. This is known as a sixty-day *GTC limit order* (GTC = good till canceled).

Limit orders are useful for buyers who want to get into a stock but feel it is currently overpriced and will soon go down, or for sellers who want to divest themselves of a stock they feel is currently undervalued and due to rise. Traders also use limit orders for short-term plays, especially on volatile stocks. If a stock has a high trading volume and its price is volatile, then there is a good chance that even a same-day limit order will lead to a transaction, whereas a market order may result in less than optimal pricing.

NOTE

Buy limit orders are placed at or below current prices, and sell limit orders are placed at the current price or higher.

MY TAKE

ON MARKET AND LIMIT ORDERS: For the patient investor who's thoroughly researched a company and feels as if she knows what an appropriate stock price should be, a limit order that reflects that price is appropriate. If the investor simply likes the company and wants to make it a part of her portfolio as soon as possible, then a market order will suffice.

Stop-Loss Orders

Stop-loss orders are used mainly by investors looking to insulate themselves from particularly volatile stocks in their portfolio. Stop-loss orders hinge on a specified "stop price."

EXAMPLE

Let's say you are holding 1,000 shares of some highly volatile experimental tech stock priced at $20 per share. That is $20,000 worth of stock and you are determined not to lose it all in the event that the stock turns sour. Therefore, to protect yourself, you place a stop-loss order with your brokerage with a stop price of $16. Should the stock sink to $16 or below, a market order will be triggered and your stock will liquidate at the next available trade. Depending on the behavior of the market, the market order (triggered by the stop-loss order) may sell below or above the stop price of $16. The important thing to know is that as soon as the stock touches the stop price, your brokerage will automatically hunt down the first and best available sale price.

Stop-loss orders can, of course, also be used by buyers when they want to get in on a particular stock when it begins to move up.

Company H is scheduled to release their earnings report for the previous quarter and you believe they are due to report better-than-expected earnings (known as a "positive earnings surprise"). You may want to put a *buy* stop-loss order on the stock with a stop price slightly above the stock's current pre-report price. If the earnings report brings good news, as you expect it will, and the stock proceeds to climb upward, then you will have an order in place to buy the stock quickly. Hopefully, the stock will continue to climb for the rest of the trading day, and your buy stop-loss order will have rewarded you with a nice price gain.

Another type of stop order is the "***stop-limit order***," which operates just like a stop-loss order except the stop price triggers a limit order rather than a market order, giving the investor firmer control over their final trading price.

The risk inherent in the stop-limit order is that, like any other limit order, the transaction is not guaranteed to be executed. In a rapidly declining market, investors relying on a stop-limit order to exit a position (sell off a stock) may find that it was impossible to find a buyer at the specified limit price, and therefore, no sale was possible.

Broker Commissions

Brokers make their money by facilitating trades for customers and charging them a commission. This commission is usually shared between the broker and the brokerage firm. Commission charges are negotiable and if you make more frequent and larger trades, then you will find more opportunities to reduce this expense, either through direct negotiation with your broker or by searching the market for competitors willing to handle your trades for less.

Stock Splits

A ***stock split*** occurs when a company decides that it wants more shares of its stock out on the market. This is done to lower the price of a stock and to encourage a wider pool of investors to consider buying in. Companies may split their stock as a countermeasure against conglomerates' or corporate raiders' attempts to centralize power by controlling large proportions of all outstanding shares. A wider investor pool makes it more difficult for a hostile conglomerate to assert a controlling interest in the company through stock ownership.

When a company splits its stock, all current shareholder positions automatically double, triple, or otherwise boost their share count in the company.

Stock splits can come in any variety of ratios—2 for 1, 3 for 1, 5 for 2, etc.

Even though investors in the company now hold twice as many (or more) shares as they did before the split, the split does not automatically raise the total value of their holdings. Theoretically, when a stock splits, the new shares should be valued proportionate to the split. That is, if the split is 2 for 1, then the new stock will be worth 50 percent as much as the old stock. But what may happen—and why investors are generally happy to see their stock split—is a surge of upward movement in the price of the split shares, ascending toward the stock's original pre-split value. Some investors see splits as a signal to buy. The stock, at least on a very superficial level, looks a lot cheaper on the market after a split than before, and when it comes to stocks, it is unwise to discount the power of perception. Though there is no evidence that a stock split is always a positive event for shareholders, many investors find themselves happy to be holding twice as many shares, free of charge.

EXAMPLE

To get a sense of the potential impact of a stock split, imagine that a well-known company with a high stock price like Alphabet Inc. (GOOG)—let's say that its trading at about $1,000 per share—decided to split its stock 3 for 1, bringing its per-share value to about $333. The demand (and price) for GOOG might spike big time following the split, as investors once dissuaded by the company's high stock price give GOOG a serious look. Such an event in the financial world would undoubtedly make big headlines.

Companies may also enact a reverse split of their stock, whereby outstanding shares are reduced by a particular ratio. A reverse split is not typically considered a healthy signal and may be the result of the company's attempts to artificially boost a flagging stock price.

MY TAKE

ON STOCK SPLITS: Stock splits used to be quite common, but over the past few years I haven't heard about them as much. It's like they have fallen out of fashion. Companies like Amazon, Google, and most especially Berkshire Hathaway (which in February of 2018 was trading at an astounding $307,400 per share)[11] seem content to allow their stock prices to appreciate indefinitely.

Cost Basis

While making money is definitely a good thing, you cannot lose sight of the fact that Uncle Sam is going to demand that you give him his piece of your investment profit. We will go into more depth on capital gains taxes in the "tax factor" section of chapter 3, but right now it is important that you understand how your investment profits are legally defined. In order to determine how much of a profit you officially make through the sale of any investment, you need to first know your cost basis for the investment. The *cost basis* is essentially the amount of money you spent in order to own an investment. If you purchase a $5 stock and it shoots up to $10, then your cost basis is still $5 plus any commissions or fees you paid to acquire the stock. Let's say you paid $2 in fees. Your cost basis would be $7. And if you sell your investment for $10, then you will be taxed on your $3 capital gain.

Investors occasionally run into trouble when trying to determine their cost basis for an investment purchased years or even decades ago. In many cases, the stock has split several times since the original purchase, so you cannot simply multiply the number of shares currently owned by the price of the stock on January 14, 1973 (or whenever it was that your security was purchased). In order to accurately determine your cost basis in these situations, you will need to use a finance database like Yahoo! or Google Finance to determine the price (roughly) of the security when it was purchased. *And* if you do not know how many shares were originally purchased, then you will need to find out how many times the stock split (and *how* it split: 2 for 1, 3 for 1, etc.) since it was purchased. Use this data to reverse-engineer your cost basis. The Yahoo! and Google Finance databases are free to use and offer an essentially boundless range of historical data.

One of the new rules put into effect by the Economic Stabilization Act of 2008 mandated that brokerages are required to hold records of the cost basis for any stocks purchased after 2011, any mutual funds purchased after 2012, and any securities at all purchased after 2014. Most brokerage accounts' online platforms make it pretty easy to identify your cost basis for most any position.

Key Stock Market Indexes

Stock market indexes come in many forms and span many markets, both domestic and international. Indexes are usually rendered as the combined, weighted average of the value of particular stock and bond assortments. Indexes may be "price weighted," like the Dow Jones Industrial Average, or "capitalization weighted," like the Nasdaq Composite. In a price-weighted index, higher priced stocks figure more heavily into the index's value. In capitalization-weighted indexes, the size of the company (market cap) determines how heavily it figures into the index's value. Let's take a quick look at a few of the most common domestic stock market indexes that you will encounter as a beginner-level investor.

Dow Jones Industrial Average

The Dow Jones Industrial Average (DJIA), also known as "the Dow," is the most recognizable of stock market indexes. The Dow originated in 1896 and was named after Charles Dow, a businessman and editor for the *Wall Street Journal*. The DJIA is generated by the performance of thirty large publicly traded companies and uses a scaling system to account for stock splits and other adjustments that would distort a standard calculation of the average stock value of its thirty component companies. In other words, the DJIA index is not really an "average" mathematically speaking, but a tracking index designed to output a consistent and meaningful relative measurement of core stock market players.

S&P 500

Like the Dow, the S&P 500 index measures the performance of US stocks. The S&P 500, as the name implies, tracks 500 stocks (whereas the Dow tracks only 30). Both the S&P 500 and the Dow are owned and operated by the same joint venture: the S&P Dow Jones Indices. Created in 1957, the S&P 500 was the first capitalization-weighted index. Because the S&P encompasses a broad range of large-cap, it is widely considered the most substantial and meaningful of major stock market indexes. Though not as widely known as the 500, there are several other S&P indexes, such as the S&P MidCap 400, the S&P SmallCap 600, and the S&P Composite 1500. Like the main S&P 500 index, these subsidiaries are all capitalization-weighted.

Nasdaq Composite

Unlike the Dow and the S&P, the Nasdaq Composite index only measures stocks that are traded on the Nasdaq Stock Market. The Nasdaq Stock Market (commonly referred to as "the Nasdaq") is separate from the New York Stock Exchange and conducts its trading through a telecommunications network rather than on a physical trading floor. The types of stocks traded on the Nasdaq (and tracked by the Nasdaq Composite) are generally tech stocks. Here you will find companies like Apple, Microsoft, and Amazon.

Fun Facts
About the Dow

Despite being created as an "industrial average"— the original DJIA included an assortment of quintessential "industrial" companies, specializing in leather, rubber, steel, cattle, gas, etc.—the current stocks that comprise the Dow are not categorically "industrial" stocks but a mix of tech, finance, retail, and pharmaceuticals.

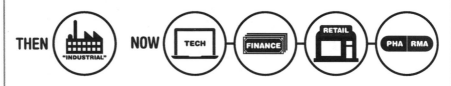

fig. 13

For a long time, GE was the last remaining DJIA company that also held a spot in the original DJIA of 1896. GE was removed from the DJIA in June of 2018.

The original DJIA was a straightforward average price of the 12 stocks that first comprised the index. As these stocks, over time, split or underwent other adjustments, the divisor in the average was modified in response. The DJIA is now properly termed a "scaled average." The current divisor used to calculate the value of the Dow is less than zero, which makes the Dow's value greater than the combined prices of all its component stocks.

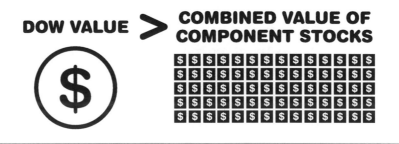

Major indices like the Dow and the S&P 500 incorporate some Nasdaq stocks (like Apple and Microsoft), but the Nasdaq Composite index does not incorporate stocks that trade only on the New York Stock Exchange.

Rather than relying on a sample pool, the Nasdaq Composite index takes into account *all 3,000-plus* stocks that trade on the Nasdaq Stock Market. Another index, known as the Nasdaq 100, measures the performance of the 100 largest nonfinancial stocks that trade on the Nasdaq. Both the Nasdaq Composite and the Nasdaq 100 are capitalization-weighted indexes.

The Russell Indexes

There are three Russell indexes. The Russell 1000® measures the performance of large-cap stocks. The Russell 2000® measures the performance of US small-cap stocks. And the Russell 3000® combines all the stocks featured in the 2000 and 1000 indexes into one master index. Of all the Russell indexes, the 2000 is the most widely used, as it is the go-to index for tracking US small-cap securities.

Other Indexes

There are a multitude of stock indexes and markets in the United States and throughout the world. The trading of stocks, bonds, and other securities happens around the clock. Because of the persistent forces of globalization, markets across the world are highly interconnected and routinely influence one another.

ON MARKET INDEXES: When assessing overall market strength, the S&P 500, rather than the Dow Jones Industrial Average, is a better across-the-board reference point, in my opinion. There are not only more companies represented in the S&P, but there is also a broader range of industrial sectors.

Bull & Bear Markets

Stock markets tend to gain in value over time, but the road to prosperity is not without turbulence. When the market goes down it often does so relatively suddenly, like in 2008 when the Dow lost 777 points in a single trading day. When the market ascends, it is usually a gradual, slow build.

A bear market is so named to evoke the bear's habit of hibernation. A bear market is a down market. Investors are selling off their stocks, putting their money in hibernation rather than exposing it to risk. A bull market is an up market. The bull charges forward and bucks and thrusts its horns upward. Investors are charging forward and using the stock market to put their money to work for them.

Typically, a market must fall by 20 percent before it is properly deemed a bear market. Sometimes, a sudden collapse of value may be attributed to a *market correction*, rather than the onset of a true bear market. A market correction is the result of inflated stock prices, improperly perceived variables, earnings reports that fail to meet expectations, or other mitigating factors that have left many investors overestimating the market's strength. Opportunities abound in both the bull and the bear markets. In the next chapter, we will take a look at some of the resources investors use to evaluate and capitalize on opportunities in the stock market.

HANDS-ON LEARNING: For a step-by-step walk through of how to use a standard trading platform to assess bid and ask prices as well purchase and sell stocks, check out my online course. More information and a discount code for the course are available at the front of the book.

Chapter Recap

» A multitude of different securities compete for your investment dollars, each offering a distinct set of risk/reward possibilities.

» Information about stocks is communicated via stock symbols and stock tables, using a number of metrics, such as price, P/E ratio, and dividend yield.

» Stocks can usually be bought or sold somewhere between their current bid and ask prices.

» The choice of market versus limit orders gives investors the option to prioritize transaction expediency over preferred price or vice versa.

» The collective performance of markets and benchmark stocks is catalogued and reported by market indexes such as the Dow Jones Industrial Average, the S&P 500, and several others.

| 2 |

From Brokerages to Robo-Advisors
How to Choose Your Investment Services

Chapter Overview
» Investment Advisors – Understanding Commissions & Credentials
» Online Investment Advisors
» Robo-Advisors
» Stock Market Apps

Planning is bringing the future into the present, so that you can do something about it now.

– ALAN LAKEIN

As a beginner-level investor, especially if you plan on putting significant sums of your money into investments, you should not try to go it alone. Too many books, blogs, and TV personalities try to convince investors that, thanks to their ironclad advice, the services of a financial advisor are no longer needed. And this message resonates, because people tend to be naturally skeptical of their financial advisor's usefulness. "Why do I keep paying them?" they may ask. "I would have made more money if I had taken all of my assets and put them in that mining stock I was scoping out last year." And maybe you would have, but that does not mean that it was a wise or sensible investment at the time.

The financial services industry is brimming with products and services claiming to provide investors with support, advice, and opportunities; and yes, many of these offerings are overpriced and hardly useful. Nevertheless, getting the right help at the right time from the right party could make a world of difference both for your portfolio and for your overall comfort with the market.

It is an interesting time in the financial services industry. Robo-advisors are making a big commotion in the marketplace, offering algorithm-based portfolio rebalancing and other financial management services. Is the financial advisor profession becoming antiquated? Is it time to take my thirty years of industry experience and call it a day? For many reasons—several of which I will share with you in this chapter—I believe the answer is no. Though robo-advisors certainly offer compatible utility for some investors, many others undoubtedly benefit from a human touch. It turns out that certain of the intricacies, uncertainties, and anomalies that go into financial planning cannot be duly serviced by ready-made advice derived from a basic risk tolerance questionnaire.

Your choice of investment services depends on a multitude of factors, including (but not limited to) the following concerns:
- » The amount of money you want to invest
- » Whether you are investing to procure shorter or longer-term gains
- » The frequency with which you wish to make trades and otherwise engage with your investment activities
- » The level of risk you are comfortable assuming
- » Your tax situation

In this chapter, we will review some of the avenues available in the pursuit of good quality investment services.

Finding a Financial Advisor

The search for a knowledgeable and trustworthy financial advisor can be difficult. You are looking for someone you can trust, someone whose personality, values, and philosophies reflect your own. Financial advisors are required to disclose their compensation structures to their clients. If a prospective advisor has not made this disclosure, don't be shy about asking for it. Many advisors and stockbrokers derive their commissions from trade volume. The more you, the client, buy or sell in the market, the more money they earn. Some advisors work on an hourly basis rather than on commission. Others collect fees derived from a fixed percentage of the assets they manage. There is no right or wrong way for a stockbroker/advisor to collect payment, provided it is fair and fully transparent. What is most important is finding someone you trust, who exhibits competence, and who you believe will safeguard your best interests.

Let's take a closer look at some of the industry titles and certifications you are likely to come across as you shop for the perfect advisor.

Investment Advisors

The term "investment advisor" was enshrined formally by the US government after the financially and otherwise tumultuous 1930s. A series of laws were passed, including the Investment Advisors Act of 1940. These laws led to the creation of the *SEC (Securities and Exchange Commission)* which would provide the federal government with a way to supervise and regulate the securities industry. In accordance with the Investment Advisors Act, investment advisors were required to register with the SEC and report their own personal assets. Once registered, these financial advisors were free to adopt the title "Registered Investment Advisor," or RIA.

RIAs (usually referred to simply as "investment advisors") often avoid conflict of interest charges by taking a standard flat fee and perhaps additional fee compensation directly related to the growth of the assets under their management. Investment advisors may also be given discretionary authority over the accounts they manage, meaning they are permitted to purchase or sell assets without the immediate consent of their clients. These discretionary privileges must be conferred in writing and specifically authorized by the client.

Certified Financial Planners (CFP®)

Of all the fancy letters to appear after the name of a financial advisor, CFP® is considered the most significant, according to the *Wall Street Journal*.[12] The Certified Financial Planner Board of Standards Inc. was established as a nonprofit in 1985. Its purpose was to integrate knowledge about the financial planning industry and to provide the public with a reliable way to qualify and evaluate prospective financial advisors. CFPs are guaranteed to possess at least a bachelor's degree, have passed a series of exams on financial planning, and have at least three years of experience working in a field related to finance. Furthermore, in order to remain certified, the CFP® Board of Standards requires ongoing coursework. CFPs who are found to be in breach of their fiduciary responsibilities to their clients are disciplined by the board, and the board ensures that all CFP® disciplinary histories are available to the public.

The web domain "LetsMakeAPlan.org" is used by the CFP® Board of Standards as a CFP® directory. You can search by location and get useful details about the CFPs in your area, such as their areas of specialty and the minimum quantity of investable assets they are prepared to handle.

On Being Selective

Be sure to interview at least three prospective financial advisors, even if you really like the first person you meet with. Ask for references, and use them. Ask for details about pay structure. Are they paid on commission or on a fee-based structure? Or are they paid in some hybrid fashion, part fee-based, part commission-based? Think about whether their pay structure will make it easier or more difficult for them to consistently act in your best interests.

Trust but verify. If your prospective financial advisor claims to be a CFP®, be sure to look him or her up on the CFP® Board of Standards website. Disciplinary history and any ethics violations should show up on the CFP® Board listings as well as on BrokerCheck.Finra.org.

 FINRA stands for Financial Industry Regulatory Authority. They are an independent nonprofit watchdog group overseen by the SEC. They are also the largest self-regulated organization (SRO) in the US securities industry.

You also have every right to request an ethics code from any prospective financial advisor. The ethics code should emphatically enumerate the *fiduciary responsibilities* the advisor assumes that oblige him to work on behalf of your best financial interests. "Fiduciary" is one of two main standards of responsibility in the world of financial advising. An advisor holding fiduciary responsibility is legally committed to recommending (and making, when authorized) investment choices that are in your best interest, in light of your circumstances and rational investment objectives. The other responsibility standard is known as "suitability." Investment advisors who adhere to this standard rather than the fiduciary standard are required to select investments suitable for you, but not necessarily in your best interest. All RIAs and CFPs carry fiduciary responsibilities.

Different financial advisors offer different types of service. If you are in need of not just investment support, but other financial services as well (insurance, tax services, estate planning, retirement, business planning) then you will make life a lot easier on yourself by finding that one qualified, ethical financial professional whom you can trust. In the event that you are looking for more multifaceted advice—investment and insurance planning, perhaps—then you should be more open to the idea of working with a financial professional who generates at least part of his or her income from transaction-based commissions derived from not one, but many different companies. The alternative is to work with what is known in the industry as a "captive agent," who, as a condition of employment, is only permitted to broker products for customers through one company.

As an independent CFP® practitioner, I relish the freedom to choose from among hundreds of companies when seeking out the best fit for my clients' needs, whether those needs be primarily investment-related or require other financial planning services, such as insurance, business, tax, retirement, and estate planning. This breadth and synchrony of selection when brokering client services is one area where we humans retain a formidable advantage over our robotic counterparts.

I find if I can earn my clients' trust by treating them fairly and putting my unique and unfettered competencies to work on their behalf, then they are usually happy to do business with me on a number of fronts. This distinctly human approach to financial services makes life easier for my clients and helps me cultivate a healthy and reputable practice. The fact that I love my work is an added bonus.

We are going to keep the promos to a minimum here, I promise, but if you are curious about my personal practice, please visit my website at SnowFinancialGroup.com.

Middle Class Woes

In recent years, finding good financial management support for middle class individuals and families has proven difficult. Many financial advisors do not want to spend the time to personally manage a portfolio worth only $50,000 or even $100,000. I hear horror stories of lower-net-worth investors having their queries directed to outsourced call centers by brokerage firms who want to focus all their prime energies only on high-value accounts. Some firms will not even take clients who have less than half a million dollars to invest, and if they do, they are sure to charge higher fees for the same services.[13] No, life is not always fair. Perhaps that is why many middle class investors have turned to self-management: independent research, facilitated by the wisdom of friends, professional associates, and publications like this one.

There are financial service companies that cater specifically to middle class investors and offer reasonable frameworks for doing business. I have personally found that working with flexible payment structures that accommodate different portfolio sizes is well worth the effort. And I am surely not the only one. It is indeed possible for middle class investors to find sound and valuable support in the industry. They just need to be aware that a lot of firms and individual advisors pursue business models that focus primarily on higher value portfolios. Do not be discouraged. Once you find the right advisor for you, then hopefully you will not ever have to go through the process again, at least not for a long while.

Internet-Based Investment Services

The vast majority of trading is conducted over the internet. Even very traditional investment services companies, such as Vanguard, Charles Schwab, and Fidelity, facilitate and encourage their customers to use online trading. Meanwhile, a whole subindustry of online brokers have taken the online trading experience to the next level by introducing powerful and affordable trading platforms that conduct nearly the entirety of their business activities in virtual spaces. Some well-known virtual traders include OptionsXpress, E-Trade (OptionsHouse), TD Ameritrade, and Scottrade. Many of these companies, such as TD Ameritrade and Scottrade, accompany their online offerings with a long-standing traditional brick-and-mortar presence as well.

Most investors, when shopping for an online broker, are going to pay attention to the costs of trading on various platforms, particularly commission costs. Just like traditional brokers, online brokers expect traders to pay a commission for the securities trades facilitated by the brokerage. They are free to charge whatever they want, but it is usually in the range of $5 to $10 per trade.

Another important factor to consider is the ease of use of the online trading platform and the ease of use of any associated apps. TopTenReviews.com[14] has a listing and ranking of twelve of the most popular online trading services on the market, complete with pricing for each service. The pros and cons of each site are reviewed, and the site makes it easy to compare platforms.

If you already have an IRA (individual retirement account), then you may be able to open up a separate brokerage (trading) account with the company that holds your IRA.

For some online investment accounts, a minimum quantity of assets is required to open an account. Do not worry if you are unsure of which brokerage is the best fit for you. There are a lot to choose from, and you can always cancel your account and transfer to another company if you find you do not like the interface, commission structure, or other attributes of any given online brokerage. Some online brokerages give new customers a batch of commission-free trades to get started with.

If you choose to forgo an advisor altogether and to rely primarily on internet-based services for your money management and investment needs, please do proceed with caution. In the early part of my career, before internet-based trading existed, I worked for an enterprise that billed itself as (and truly was) a "discount brokerage." The convenience and low-cost services we offered were the equivalent of what internet-based investment services are today. Customers came to us because they wanted to manage their own portfolios, make their own trades, etc. In return, we took a very modest transaction-based commission. Our business model emphasized a consummate laissez-faire approach, giving customers minimal advice and maximum freedom over their investment choices. Such an approach, however, proved to be a difficult task for me at times, as I had to stand by and watch customers make poor and life-altering money management decisions. The consequences of some of these decisions were often irrevocable, even tragic. Behaving prudently in the marketplace is not always an intuitive inclination. For example, when we see a stock going down in value, our intuition will often urge us to sell—get out and salvage as much value as you can! Hurry, before you lose any more! I watched helplessly as this panic mentality overtook so many investors in down markets. Left to their own devices, many investors seem to have an unfortunate knack for selling at the bottom of the market and buying at the top, when they should of course be doing the opposite. Bottom line, think carefully before you decide to go it alone in the marketplace, and do not underestimate the value of an experienced professional in your corner.

Internet-Based Options Trading Services

You may notice that a lot of the popular online brokerages include the term "options" in their title. Even E-Trade released a spin-off service called "OptionsHouse," presumably so they could catch the attention of the many traders who are specifically looking for a place to trade options. Take note, though, many brokerages trade options, even those that do not include the word "options" in their titles. We will discuss the trading of options in greater detail in chapter 6 (and you can finally see what all the fuss is about). Beginner-level investors, especially those who are not seeking to engage in higher risk trades right out of the gate, should focus on evaluating and purchasing stocks and other securities. Options, futures, and short selling are more complicated and risky investment instruments and are not ideal for newcomers.

Robo-Advisors

Robo-advisors are an emerging trend in investing, whereby the expense of a human financial advisor may be reduced by relying instead on a computerized algorithm. A customer's responses to a basic risk assessment questionnaire are often used as the input for these algorithms. The output is a prepackaged investment model coordinated to match the customer's risk tolerance and investment objectives. Major investment management companies, such as Charles Schwab, Fidelity, TD Ameritrade, and E-Trade have joined the robo-advisor movement. However, some of the most innovative and competent robo-advisor services are offered by lesser-known companies like Wealthfront and Betterment.

Robo-advisors use sophisticated computer algorithms to analyze your investment portfolio and make recommendations. Among the competencies of a robo-advisor is the ability to **rebalance** a portfolio (reconfiguring asset allocation to achieve a desired proportion of various investments). A good robo-advisor will also offer a "tax-loss harvesting" feature, which allows investors to sell failing investments and offset the losses against the sale of investments with gains.

Over a given period, Jennifer has $30,000 worth of realized capital losses from the sale of a poorly performing mutual fund, but she has a similar $30,000 worth of realized capital gains from the sale of another much better performing mutual fund. Using *tax-loss harvesting*, Jennifer can use the $30,000 in losses to offset the tax liability incurred by the $30,000 in gains. Both securities must be sold during the course of the same tax year. This type of tax-loss harvesting can be utilized to an unlimited degree each year to claim tax deductions and may be applied to losses from any investment security, not just mutual funds.

The IRS has a rule known as the "wash-sale rule" that prohibits investors from repurchasing within thirty days the same or similar securities that were sold for the purpose of obtaining a tax deductible capital loss. If the seller fails to wait for at least thirty days before repurchasing the security, then no tax write-off is permitted.

Because the robo-advisor space is one of the industry's latest innovations, there are countless promotions available for customers willing to give it a try. The consulting firm A.T. Kearney published a study in 2015 forecasting widespread adoption of the robo-advisor model in the near future.[15]

Compared to the standard 1 percent fee charged by a flesh-and-blood financial advisor, customers will forfeit only .25 to .5 percent of their total portfolio value to take advantage of a robo-advisor's platform. There are a couple of free robo-advisors on the market (Charles Schwab and WiseBanyan at the moment), though each comes with a snag. WiseBanyan offers tax-loss harvesting as an add-on service, at a cost of .25 percent of your account value.

Schwab requires that you have $50,000 invested before they will provide tax-loss harvesting support.[16]

Potential robo-advisor customers should also be aware of the fact that brokerages that offer both robo-advisory services and their own funds, such as Schwab and Fidelity, may configure robo-advisor algorithms to feature their own proprietary funds more prominently. They may even attempt to configure these algorithms to direct customers toward funds with higher fees and expense ratios (the things that make them money). Remember, at the end of the day, a robo-advisor does exactly what it is told and has no capacity to genuinely care about your interests or your future. If a robo-advisor algorithm is pushing you into expensive funds, then you are looking at paying an extra .5 to 2 percent on your investments. Add that to the robo-advisor's .25 to .5 percent account management fee, and suddenly the human financial advisor's 1 percent fee may not seem so bad after all.

Betterment and Wealthfront are examples of companies that offer robo-advisor services and *do not* also offer proprietary funds. Companies like these, without any skin in the game, may in the long run be better for consumers. Also, if you are looking to minimize fees, you may want to look at robo-advisors that offer algorithms favoring ETFs or low-cost mutual funds.

The Case for Staying Human

It is important not to underestimate the value of financial planning, a task that for many investors may be best supported by a human financial advisor. Your investments change over time, and the composition of your portfolio must continually accommodate a multitude of factors including your proximity to retirement, college savings accounts for your children, and realistic contingencies for market downturns.

Some financial advisors spend several hours interviewing their clients before beginning work on an appropriate investment strategy. As client intake goes, our process, relative to that of the robots, is considerably more substantive than filling out an online form. A deeper understanding of their clients' investment objectives can make human advisors more optimally equipped to support a greater breadth of client needs, including estate planning, insurance, and more complex tax management consulting.

The last thing I will say on this subject is also one of the most difficult things to talk about. Human financial advisors can be an invaluable counterbalance for bad financial behavior. This is difficult to talk about because most people like to think that they have good sensibilities when it comes to managing their money. But after spending thirty years in the financial services industry, I am left with an unenviable obligation to report the truth—many people are poor managers of their investments and personal finances.

Don't take my word for it, though. All you have to do is look at down market versus up market investment trends and data. When securities lose value, people sell them off when they should be buying them. And when securities gain value, people buy them when they should be selling them off.

Recent Proof of a "Buy High & Sell Low" Mentality

INVESTMENT PATTERNS AT THE WRONG TIMES

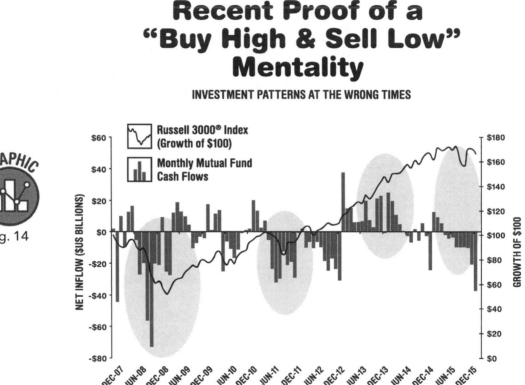

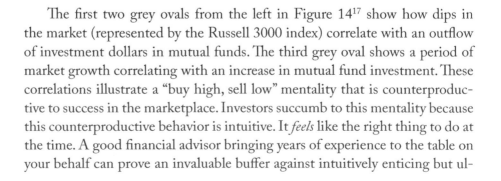

fig. 14

The first two grey ovals from the left in Figure 14[17] show how dips in the market (represented by the Russell 3000 index) correlate with an outflow of investment dollars in mutual funds. The third grey oval shows a period of market growth correlating with an increase in mutual fund investment. These correlations illustrate a "buy high, sell low" mentality that is counterproductive to success in the marketplace. Investors succumb to this mentality because this counterproductive behavior is intuitive. It *feels* like the right thing to do at the time. A good financial advisor bringing years of experience to the table on your behalf can prove an invaluable buffer against intuitively enticing but ultimately poor financial judgment calls. More plainly put—do not undervalue the simple luxury of having someone in your corner to talk to when you need a little reassurance.

The markets have an impeccable, 100 percent track record when it comes to recovery, but during a down economy, when you are watching your portfolio decline in value, it can be difficult to act out of historical awareness rather than out of panic.

Robot vs. Human
THE ADVISOR WARS OF THE 21ST CENTURY

fig. 15

Robo-Advisor

Key Attributes:

- Lower fees (.25% to .5%)

- Pre-packaged investment-only plans

- May give undue prominence to expensive proprietary funds

- May offer tax-loss harvesting

Human Advisor

Key Attributes:

- Standard fee is 1%

- Comprehensive & personal investment plans

- May offer tax management and other financial services

- A buffer against "bad financial behavior"

Follow and Trade Stocks with Mobile Apps

Well before the iPhone, mobile phones were equipped with simplistic web browsers that could access a limited array of content. Among these earliest of mobile web functions was the ability to get up-to-date information on stock prices. That functionality now comes standard with pre-installed stock tracking apps on most smartphones. In addition to those that come pre-installed, there are now an abundance of apps to choose from that will allow you not only to track but to trade. Such a convenience likely goes underappreciated by investment newcomers, but not by those of us who remember the hassle of phoning in trades and waiting on hold until a broker was available, all while watching the stock we were trying to sell plummet to new and costly depths.

Most investment services offer their customers a mobile app they can use to view and trade stocks at the touch of a screen. Your investment services app should also give you the option of setting up email alerts to notify you when stocks you are following reach a certain price point. If you are looking to buy into a stock but feel confident that its price will decrease in upcoming weeks or months, then setting up an email alert can ensure that you do not miss your buying opportunity should your prediction prove accurate.

For the purpose of simply following stocks, basic pre-installed smartphone stock apps offer a convenient, minimalist solution. These apps are often customizable, allowing you to follow the performance of most any stock. You can also use these apps to follow the performance of other investment vehicles, like foreign currency and treasuries.

Some smartphone stock apps have fifteen-minute delays on information unless you upgrade to the premium service.

Stock apps may have more functionality than meets the eye. Try holding your smartphone sideways; the app may automatically convert to a new interface that will allow you to browse performance data for your selected stocks and other securities.

Here are a few other noteworthy app-based smartphone concepts that new investors may appreciate:

» **Scan product barcodes** – Did an innovative product catch your eye on your last shopping trip? Some stock apps offer a bar code scanning function, which allows users to identify the publicly traded company behind any product.

- » **Get breaking news** – Some stock apps provide the latest news about any stock or security you are following.

- » **Explore stock "heat maps"** – Heat map functionality allows investors to visualize the big winners and losers of the market in real time via a collection of sector-specific "heat maps" that show who's hot and who's not.

- » **Try virtual investing** – Jump into the stock market risk-free with a virtual investing (often called virtual trading) app. Virtual trading can be useful for beginner-level traders or for those who want to simulate the experience of throwing serious money around without having to jump out of a high-rise window in the event of their investments going bad.

- » **Get social in the marketplace** – Some stock apps provide a social, twitter-like platform for their users. You can exchange tips with other members and assess how bullish or bearish the community is on a given asset.

Chapter Recap

- » CFP® status, a clean disciplinary record, and stated acceptance of fiduciary responsibility give credibility to a prospective financial advisor.

- » The vast majority of trading is conducted online, and a multitude of online trading platforms vie for market share.

- » Robo-advisors use computerized portfolio management algorithms to provide consumers with lower-cost financial advice.

- » Both iOS and Android offer several unique trading apps that can make your experience as an investor more informative and more fun.

| 3 |
How to Use Time to Your Advantage
Grow Your Wealth & Fund the Perfect Retirement

Chapter Overview
» Returns on Investment
» Types of Stocks
» Mutual Funds and ETFs
» Investment Taxes

Compound interest is the eighth wonder of the world. He who understands it earns it; he who doesn't pays it.

– ALBERT EINSTEIN

In the world of investing, one of the most treasured assets is time. This is why your parents, as retirement pressed in on them, urged you to start putting money away for retirement at a time when, in your view, there were a million and one more pressing matters at hand. But, as you probably have come to realize, your parents were right. The earlier your money is invested, the more time it has to accumulate compounding returns.[18]

Consider a 25-year-old who begins saving for retirement by investing $200 a month and a 35-year-old who begins investing $200 a month. Both investors earn the same annual return, about 6 percent on average. In spite of the 35-year-old's late start, he will have invested only $24,000 less than the 25-year-old by age 65. But unfortunately for the 35-year-old, his funds available at retirement will be $200,000 less than those of the 25-year-old who started early. That is the power of time.

One of the principal culprits responsible for the 25-year-old investor's success relative to that of the 35-year-old investor is the phenomenon of "compound interest." Compound interest is not terribly difficult to understand, but the extent to which its power is overlooked by the general public is remarkable. When you are paid interest, dividends, or capital gains, you will almost always have the option of reinvesting these earnings back into the principal investment. Over time, your interest earnings generate their own interest and your dividend payments begin producing their own dividends. The cumulative effect is exponential in nature and can be instrumental to your accumulation of wealth.

To illustrate the power of compound interest, let's take a look at a hypothetical investment of $500 that gains 10% in annual interest.

- Initial Investment of $500
- Compounding Interest at a Rate of 10%

fig. 16

Number of Years	Investment Worth
5	$805.26
10	$1,296.87
15	$2,088.62
20	$3,363.75
25	$5,417.35
30	$8,724.70
35	$14,051.22
40	$22,629.63
45	$36,445.24

After 45 years, thanks to compound interest, a $500 investment left untouched is now worth $36.5K. For the 25-year-old investor looking to retire at or around age 70, the ability to leverage compound interest is extremely powerful.

One popular and very simple approach to calculating returns on investments which accumulate compound interest is to utilize "the Rule of 72." The Rule of 72 states that if you divide the number 72 by your compound annual interest rate you will get the total number of years required to double your money.

Let's go back to our $500 investment in Figure 16. If we want to calculate how long it would take to double our money to $1,000 we would make the following calculation:

fig. 17

$$72 \div 10 = \boxed{\text{The number of years required to } \underline{\text{double}} \text{ the principal at a compound annual interest rate of 10\%}} = 7.2 \text{ Yrs}$$

Understanding Returns

The return made on any investment is determined by comparing the current value of the investment with the original value of the investment. The strength of a return is thus normally expressed as a percentage value and is calculated as follows:

$$\frac{\text{(CURRENT VALUE OF THE INVESTMENT} - \text{ORIGINAL VALUE OF THE INVESTMENT)}}{\text{(ORIGINAL VALUE OF THE INVESTMENT)}}$$

A stock bought in 2017 for $30 that is worth $90 in 2035 has a return of 200 percent.

$$(\$90 - \$30) / \$30 = 200\%$$

If an investment issues a dividend or other yield, then that too must be calculated into the return formula:

$$\frac{\text{(CURRENT VALUE OF THE INVESTMENT} - \text{ORIGINAL VALUE OF THE INVESTMENT)} + \text{YIELD}}{\text{(ORIGINAL VALUE OF THE INVESTMENT)}}$$

A stock bought in 2017 for $80 is worth $155 in 2025 and has yielded a total of $5 per share in dividend payments. The return is 100%.

$$((\$155 - \$80) + \$5) / \$80 = 100\%$$

In addition to calculating returns on an individual stock or bond, or on a portfolio as a whole, returns are calculated on entire stock indexes, such as the Dow and the S&P 500. These "total returns," as they are called, though calculated daily, are usually published monthly, quarterly, and annually. To calculate the total return on an index, the change in the total value of the index is measured over a specified length of time (usually a month or a year). Any dividends issued (yields) are factored into the final value of the index and the result is usually expressed as a percentage value: "The total return on the Dow was 5.1 percent last year."

The reason total returns are important, especially for beginner-level investors, is that they provide a way to assess the historical behavior of the market. Analysts report that if we average out all the annual returns of the stock market, beginning in 1802, we will find an average annual return of 8.3 percent.[19] This average changes as we move through epochs of time. Since 1926, for example, the average annual return from the stock market has been 10.1 percent. Figure 18[20] shows the stock market returns, positive and negative, since 1929.

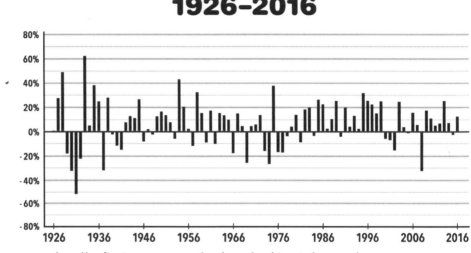

DOW Yearly Return
1926–2016

fig. 18

source: http://tradinginvestment.com/stock-market-historical-returns/

For a beginner-level investor with the long term in mind, it is essential to understand how the stock market behaves over long stretches of time. Such an understanding will ensure that you do not panic and make a disastrous sell-off during a down year after being shocked by the dramatic decline in your portfolio's net worth. The market will go down at points, undoubtedly, but it will also recover and grow back stronger. Successful long-term investors must take it as an article of faith that the market will learn from its mistakes.

ON HOW TO MAXIMIZE RETURNS: I urge my clients to avoid selling into weakness. Instead, I encourage them to *buy* into weakness. When bear markets emerge, it is actually a great buying opportunity, and when stocks are charging along bullishly, you may want to to think about selling some off. When selling into a strong market, the proceeds can be used to rebalance your portfolio, making sure you are holding onto an appropriate asset mix (discussed later in this chapter). It is also a good time to take a look at some stocks that are not doing so well and to buy into them when they appear the weakest. Simply put, *buy into weakness and sell into strength.*

Accounting for Inflation

Inflation is a concept that most people understand—it is the decline in a currency's purchasing power. More money is required over time to purchase the same amount of goods or services. What most people do not understand, however, are the causes of inflation. And what practically no one understands is the persistence of inflation over time. Let's start with the causes. One cause of inflation is demand outpacing the supply of goods and services being generated in the economy.

> If the aggregate marketing efforts of smartphone manufacturers drive up demand for the latest smartphone models, so much so that the industry is unable to produce enough product to satisfy this demand, then the cost of smartphones may go up. More dollars may be needed to purchase the same product.

Another cause of inflation is independent of demand: a rise in the cost of producing goods.

> If new trade policy limits the ability of the smartphone manufacturer to source its parts and labor from China, then the costs of producing the new smartphone will rise, as will the price.

Inflation can also occur if something restricts the supply of a good, service, or commodity.

> A massive labor strike obstructs the ability of the smartphone manufacturer to ship its new smartphone to customers. The strike may drive shipping prices higher, which in turn inflates the cost of obtaining the new smartphone.

Smartphones and other consumer goods are not the only products subject to inflation. Stocks, for instance, can inflate as well, sometimes dramatically.

During the "tech bubble" of the early 2000s, the hype surrounding tech stocks was so berserk that demand skyrocketed, causing the prices of the stocks to inflate severely. The tech bubble phenomenon was not caused by a limited supply of goods (there was plenty of tech stock to go around) but the demand side was so insatiable that it forced prices upward, for a while. Once the bubble popped, tech stock prices came tumbling down to earth.

To summarize, inflation can be caused by a handful of economic factors and can lead to either long- or short-term increases in the price of goods and services. Deflationary pressures in the economy (prices being driven down) are often more complex than inflationary pressures. In the short term, when deflation is setting in, it is often very difficult to trace the movements of the "invisible hand," so to speak, and to explain exactly what is happening and why, at least until we get a longer view of the phenomenon. In other words, the causes of deflation become clearer over an extended timeline.

Though the reasons are not abundantly clear (nor within the scope of this book to explain) inflation is persistent over long periods of time in almost all economies. The one hundred thousand dollars you have in your bank account will purchase more goods and services today than they will purchase fifty years from now. We can attribute some of inflation's persistence to the actions of central banks around the world. These are government-sponsored entities which have a mandate to see inflation increase at a slow and steady pace, conducive to a healthy and growing economy (see *The Inflation Risk* section in chapter 1).

So what does inflation mean to you as an investor? Since the persistence of inflation is a relevant economic force, long-term (and short-term) investors would be remiss not to factor inflation into their retirement planning and other investment decisions.

Going back to our long view of the stock market, the average rate of return on the stock market since 1802 (8.3 percent annually) is mitigated by the average rate of inflation (1.4 percent annually). Therefore our true return must subtract the inflation rate (8.3% − 1.4%) in order for us to arrive at the truest rate of return (6.9 percent).

The average annual inflation rate since 1926 has been about 3 percent; therefore, even though the average return from the stock market is 10.1 percent, the true appreciation of stock market value is 7.1 percent. A lot of financial institutions recommend that you assume a 3 percent inflation rate when planning for retirement. Keep in mind, however, that if you look at year-by-year inflation you will see a wide range of data, from 14.4 percent (1947) to -9.9 percent (1932). The rate of inflation, like the stock market, is both volatile and persistently positive over time.

The Rule of 72—explained earlier in this chapter as a simple method by which one may calculate the time required to double an investment's worth at a given compound interest rate—can also be used to calculate the diminishing impact of inflation:

GRAPHIC

fig. 19

72 ÷ (The Rate of Inflation) = | **The number of years required to diminish by ½ the purchasing power of a given dollar amount**

EXAMPLE

If we assume an average inflation rate of 3 percent, then it would take 24 years (72 ÷ 3) for $1,000 (or any amount) to lose half of its purchasing power.

CAUTION

Inflation is a particularly noteworthy threat to retirees relying heavily on investment-based fixed incomes such as bonds, annuity payments, or pensions. These income sources do not usually rise in value and therefore are defenseless against inflation. This is part of the reason why I recommend that even retirees keep a healthy portion of their assets in stocks.

Determining an Appropriate Asset Mix

One of the key questions you and your financial advisor must answer when constructing and maintaining your long-term portfolio is the question of asset mix. What types of investments do you want to make, in what quantity, and at what proportion. A long-term portfolio can consist of any number of different asset types: stocks, bonds, mutual funds, ETFs, etc.

Advisors use a variety of general rules to help their clients allocate assets appropriately in light of their unique investment objectives. One of the core questions likely to arise during any discussion of asset allocation is, "What proportion of my assets should be kept in stocks versus bonds and other securities?"

To get a sense of how this question might be resolved for any given investor, let's compare stock returns over time with bond returns. If we look only at long-term bonds (the longer the term, the higher the yield) since 1926, we find an average annual return of 5.5 percent. Since our inflation rate for this period is 3 percent, we are left with a net return on investment of 2.5 percent annually. Recall that our net return for stocks since 1926 averaged out to 7.1 percent. Stocks are more volatile than bonds, however, so if we are getting close to retirement we do not want to risk having to wait through several years of recession with very little income. Bonds, though less liquid than stocks, offer a reliable source of income in the form of interest payments. Reliability is great, but remember, bonds can be lousy at keeping pace with inflation.

In the end it is all about striking a balance with a solid mix of assets that are well diversified and appropriate for your needs. Thankfully, given the wondrous range of securities available on the market, there are many paths to a healthy, diverse portfolio. Let's take a look at diversity within stocks in particular.

Diversity in Stocks

You have probably heard the imperative, "diversify your portfolio," more times than you can count. The idea is simple. Don't put all your eggs in one basket. There are several ways to make your portfolio flourish with a diversity to rival the great tropical rainforests. Here are a few ways you might go about pursuing balance and diversity:

» Mix *defensive* stocks with *cyclical* stocks. Defensive stocks are a particular stock type that is well insulated from the overall condition of the economy. The healthcare sector, discount retail, and food suppliers are less susceptible to poor economies. Cyclical stocks, by contrast, are hot when the market's hot, but can be severely weakened by a poor economy. Travel and tourism companies suffer in weak economies, as do automobile, tire, and auto parts manufacturers, as well as home appliance companies.

fig. 20

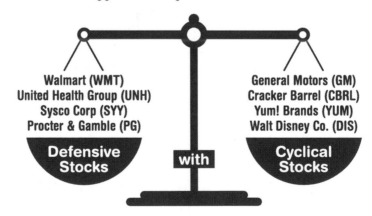

Walmart (WMT)
United Health Group (UNH)
Sysco Corp (SYY)
Procter & Gamble (PG)
Defensive Stocks

with

General Motors (GM)
Cracker Barrel (CBRL)
Yum! Brands (YUM)
Walt Disney Co. (DIS)
Cyclical Stocks

» Mix stocks of varying market cap size. The three main market cap tiers (small-cap, mid-cap, and large-cap) were broken down in detail in chapter 1. In certain conditions, smaller cap companies may perform exceedingly well across the board, while larger cap stocks falter.

The reverse may also be true at certain times. A portfolio full of large-caps could remain woefully stagnant over time, while a portfolio full of small-caps may wash away in the rain. A good portfolio holds a generally equitable mix of large-, mid-, and small-cap stocks.

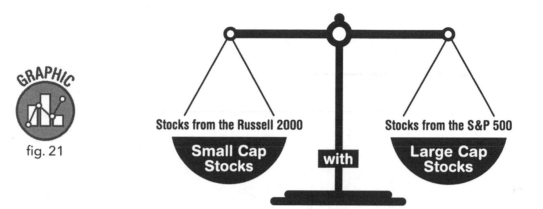

GRAPHIC

fig. 21

ON SMALL-CAP VS. LARGE-CAP: Historically speaking, a portfolio full of small companies will produce higher returns than a portfolio full of large companies.[21] Nevertheless, balancing out your portfolio with mid- and large-cap stocks can stabilize your returns and provide a cushion during difficult economic times. Also, don't put too much money in any one small-cap stock, because smaller companies can fail more easily. Consider investing in a pre-diversified mutual fund or ETF (both discussed later in this chapter) that focuses on small-cap stocks.

MY TAKE

Small Cap vs. Large Cap According to Fama/French

GRAPHIC

fig. 22

Evaluation Period	Small Cap Stocks Outperform Large Cap Stocks
1 year	57% of the time
5 year	64% of the time
10 year	72% of the time
15 year	82% of the time

Small-cap stocks historically outperform large-cap stocks

Though data in Figure 22 pertains specifically to US small-cap stocks versus US large-cap stocks, the study cited observed a similar trend in both international and emerging market small-cap stocks when compared against large-cap stocks from the same category.

» Mix *value* stocks with *growth* stocks. **Value stocks** are so named because they generally hail from strong and tested market sectors and have a low P/E ratio (see chapter 1). **Growth stocks** are those that carry a powerful and promising story. They are poised to explode in a red-hot sector. Everyone wants in and the P/E ratio is high, so the stocks are considered more expensive. But it is worth the price (or so we would like to believe) because in just a few short years the stock is going to skyrocket, and we will be glad we were aboard at the ground floor. This story may or may not come to fruition, but if you balance value stocks with growth stocks, you will get a nice mix of stability and opportunity.

GRAPHIC

fig. 23

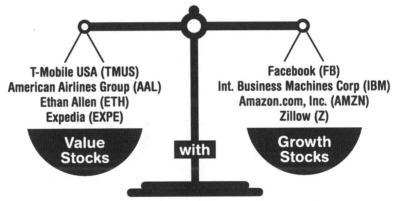

ON VALUE VS. GROWTH: Value stocks are more likely to outperform growth stocks over time, but not always.[22] A good portfolio, in my opinion, allocates more assets to value stocks than growth stocks, but still contains both types of securities.

Though data in Figure 24 pertains specifically to US value stocks versus US growth stocks, the study cited observed a similar trend in both international and emerging market value stocks when compared against growth stocks from the same category.

Value Stocks vs. Growth Stocks According to Fama/French

Evaluation Period	Value Stocks Outperform Growth Stocks
1 year	61% of the time
5 year	77% of the time
10 year	88% of the time
15 year	97% of the time

Value stocks historically outperform growth stocks

» Use *correlations*. Correlations measure the reactions of different stocks to the same factors. For example, several stocks are thought to have a high correlation with the price of oil. When oil goes up, so do the stock prices. Other securities appear to have negative correlations, such as the value of the dollar relative to the value of gold. As the dollar loses value, gold gains value. Positive and negative market correlations exist throughout the market across various sectors and are apt to change with time. A habit of good portfolio managers is to keep a mix of negatively correlated or low correlated stocks. This strategy may keep your portfolio stable while growing steadily and will make it less likely to suffer sudden across-the-board losses.

Don't forget to take advantage of the digital companion files included with your purchase of this book. Among other resources, you'll find an asset allocation spreadsheet that's easy to use and will help you develop a strong asset allocation strategy for your portfolio. Access the spreadsheet and all digital companion resources for this title at: **www.clydebankmedia.com/investing-assets**

More on Correlations

Correlations between securities are rated on a scale of -1 to +1, with -1 being perfectly non-correlated and 1 being perfectly correlated. A correlation of 0 means that there is no discernable relationship between the securities; the performance of one is not likely to have any positive or negative influence on the other. A well-diversified portfolio will contain investment correlations that range between -1 and 1. Some of your holdings undoubtedly will correlate highly with one another. That is fine, so long as you can form a counterbalance with other holdings that are more strongly non-correlated.

If your assets are too highly correlated across the board, averaging toward 1, then your entire portfolio will be subject to more risk and volatility. Small changes in one sector of the market will have the potential to dramatically affect the total value of your portfolio.

On the other hand, if your assets have a nice range of correlation values from -1 to 1, then your portfolio is likely to have more stability and less risk exposure.

fig. 25

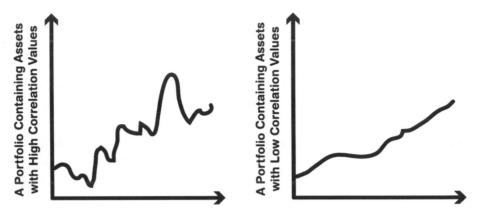

Index Investing & Mutual Funds

There are several ways to make broad, general investments that can be tracked by broad market indexes, such as the Dow and the S&P 500. You cannot, of course, invest in an index directly, but asset management companies, such as BlackRock and Vanguard, set up funds, known as *index funds*, which are composed of the various securities that comprise an index.

> A Dow Jones Industrial Average index fund would be comprised of the thirty companies that make up the DJIA index. These assets are rolled into a new product—the index fund—which can be traded as a mutual fund or an exchange traded fund (ETF).

Index funds are a type of *mutual fund* (they can also be ETFs [see the following section]). The primary utility of mutual funds is the ability of investors to instantly diversify their portfolios without having to purchase their stock à la carte. Mutual funds are created when investors pool their money together and hand it over to a fund manager who chooses an assortment of stocks, bonds, and other securities in which to invest. Many newcomers to investing cannot afford to buy a multitude of different stocks (and even if they could afford it, they might not know how to select them), so they begin their investing career by buying into mutual funds or ETFs (see below) which come pre-diversified.

Some mutual funds, like index funds, do not require the expertise of a whip-smart fund manager, as they are pegged directly to the performance of the index. These mutual funds are known as passively managed funds. You will not pay as much for them up front, because the administrative costs are low. Actively managed funds are those where you do rely on the expertise, ongoing research, and decision making of fund managers. This costs money. Hence, actively managed mutual funds are more expensive, but, in theory, should perform better over time (not always the case). Mutual funds pay out to investors in the form of income distributions and capital gains distributions. Income distributions come from the yields offered by the fund's underlying assets, that is, the dividends from the stocks and the interest from the bonds. The capital gains distributions are a result of the fund manager's decision to sell off one or more of the mutual fund's assets. At the investor's discretion, these gains may be received in cash or may be automatically reinvested in the fund. Either way, though, the government is going to claim its share in taxes. Your mutual fund company will send out paperwork, 1099-DIVs or 1099-INTs, so you can file your taxes properly.

NOTE

If a mutual fund goes down in value and you decide to sell it, the loss can be used to offset future gains (in the same year) for tax purposes.

Unlike ETFs or stocks, which fluctuate in share price throughout the day, mutual funds calculate a ***net asset value (NAV)*** at the close of each trading day. NAV is the mutual fund equivalent of a share price. It is calculated by taking the total value of the fund's portfolio (minus fees and any other liabilities) divided by the total number of outstanding shares in the fund. Consider the sample mutual fund in Figure 26.

SAMPLE MUTUAL FUND
with 300 MILLION outstanding shares

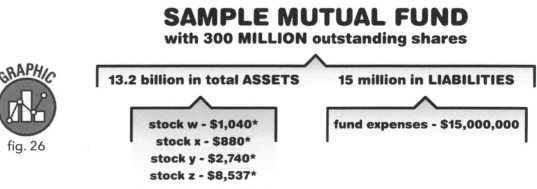

GRAPHIC

fig. 26

13.2 billion in total ASSETS

15 million in LIABILITIES

stock w - $1,040*
stock x - $880*
stock y - $2,740*
stock z - $8,537*

*worth of shares (in millions)

fund expenses - $15,000,000

The sample mutual fund's assets are comprised of only four stocks (a paucity of diversity unheard of in the real world, but this is just an example) worth a total of 13.2 billion dollars. The fund has 15 million dollars in liabilities due to fee obligations and other fund expenses. And it has 300 million shares outstanding. To calculate the fund's NAV we take the 13.2 billion, subtract 15 million, then divide by 300 million. The NAV of the mutual fund is ≈ $44— that is the per-share price you are going to pay to be an owner of this fund.

Figure 27 contains a listing of various hypothetical (not real) mutual funds. The trading symbols for mutual funds, you will notice, always have an X at the end. This is to signify that the security is a mutual fund, not to be confused with a stock. In Figure 27, the mutual fund's NAVs from the close of trading on the previous day are listed. Though not shown in Figure 27, this data is normally accompanied by the dollar and percentage change of the fund's NAV relative to its previous close (from two trading days prior to the current day).

GRAPHIC

fig. 27

Name	Symbol	NAV (per share)	Change (% change)
ABC Index Fund	AINDX	213.23	-1.07 (- 0.56%)
FundCorp Value Stock Fund	FVSFX	42.14	+0.53 (+ 1.26%)
InvestorCorp Growth Stock Fund	IVCGX	15.26	+0.02 (+ 0.13%)
ABC Biotechnology Portfolio Fund	ABIOX	20.01	-0.20 (- 1.00%)
FundCorp Retirement 2050 Fund	FRRDX	28.83	-0.23 (- 0.81%)
Investomatic Financial Index Fund	IFIXX	20.77	+0.01 (+ .05%)
JohnnyMarket's Tech Stock Fund	JOTCX	6.82	-0.05 (- 0.73%)
InvestorCorps Emerging Market Fund	ICOEX	23.64	-0.16 (- 0.68%)
ABC Low Volatility Bond Fund	ABCBX	9.68	0.00 (0.00%)

In addition to the information contained in the mutual fund listing in Figure 27, some mutual fund listings will also include the "30-day SEC yield" for the fund, which is an estimate of the fund's dividends and interest returns expressed as a 30-day average.

NOTE

You may also come across mutual fund listings that feature "SEC yields" rather than, or in addition to, "30-day SEC yields." Both stand-alone and 30-day SEC yields are an expression of what would theoretically be paid out to the investor assuming no changes were made to the fund's holdings.

The "SEC yield" is so named because the formula used to project the estimate is mandated by the SEC, to prevent fund managers from using formulas of their choice to project returns. The SEC mandate forces funds to standardize their reporting, which makes it easier for the investor to make an apples-to-apples comparison of mutual funds offered by many different companies.

The 30-day SEC yield is based on past data. It in no way guarantees that the fund will produce equivalent returns in the future. As you will see time and again in various disclaimers for financial securities, "past performance does not guarantee future results."

SEC yields are usually listed for the comparison of bond funds. When using the SEC yield to compare securities, it is important to make apples-to-apples comparisons along similar asset classes: long-term versus short-term, stocks versus bonds, etc.

Though not charted in Figure 27, another important mutual fund metric is the *expense ratio*. Management of a mutual fund is not free, especially when the fund is actively managed. Analysts have to be paid. Commissions have to be paid to brokers who buy and sell stocks on behalf of the fund. The expense ratio reflects the percentage of a fund's earnings spent on managing the fund. The higher the expense ratio, the more share values are lowered to pay for the fund's management. Expense ratios vary, usually falling in the range of somewhere between .5 percent and 3 percent.

Only a fund's fixed expenses are listed in the expense ratio. Variable expenses, such as turnover costs (the fees incurred by a mutual fund when selling off securities or buying new ones) are usually not published in an easy-to-find manner. However, there are information services, such as PersonalFund.com[23], that allow investors to assess variable expenses and elements of mutual funds' expense structures.

Mutual funds can be composed of stocks, bonds, or a mix of both. They can encapsulate a variety of market strategies and risk. Funds can even be tailored to an investor's social values (see chapter 8 on socially responsible investing). The SEC requires that a prospectus be issued for mutual funds. The *prospectus* discloses the fund's strategy, goals, and risks. It also discloses the identities of the fund's managers and advisors along with the fees and expenses associated with the fund. The SEC requires that prospectuses be submitted to a fund's shareholders and also, when requested, to investors who are considering an investment in the fund.

In addition to the general prospectus, which discloses the fees and fixed expenses associated with a fund, there is a secondary or *"part B" prospectus* that discusses variable costs, such as the trading that takes place within the fund: when the fund divests of a security and invests in others. Similarly to the limitations of a general expense ratio, the general prospectus usually does not account for these additional and often significant expenses. Part B prospectuses are usually not issued automatically like the general prospectus, but must be explicitly requested by the investor.

The majority of mutual funds on the market are "open-end funds." Shares may be sold to the public in unlimited quantities, and they are bought and sold on the basis of their NAV. Other funds are "closed-end funds," which issue only a limited number of shares. If demand grows, a closed-end fund will raise its price rather than issue new shares. The price is based on the market demand for the fund, not its NAV.

Mutual fund load refers to the commission paid to an advisor or broker for researching and selecting a mutual fund on a client's behalf. Front-end load is paid when the mutual fund is acquired, and back-end load (also known as "contingent deferred sales charge") is paid when the mutual fund is sold. Back-end loads may be reduced or eliminated if the investor holds the fund for a certain period of time. Investors who want to research and select their own mutual funds will often seek out "no-load" funds.

Many mutual funds charge a "redemption fee" to discourage investors from using mutual funds as a vehicle for short-term trading. Redemption fees are intended to prevent short-term speculators from harming the interests of other investors in the fund. When a mutual fund is bought and liquidated rapidly, it raises the expense ratio. Since you cannot just sell the fund to another buyer, the fund managers have to immediately liquidate stocks, bonds, and other securities to fulfill the sell order, which drives down performance and hurts the fund's other investors. The rapid buying and selling of mutual funds also forces the fund to maintain an ample supply of cash in order to promptly settle with the sellers. Since cash does not appreciate in value, holding a disproportionately large cash position is not in the best interest of the fund or its investors.

Exchange Traded Funds

An ***ETF (exchange traded fund)*** is something of a hybrid between a mutual fund and a stock. Like stocks, ETFs always trade on the open market. If you watch CNBC or another financial news network, you will see ETFs floating along the ticker. Like mutual funds, ETFs can be comprised of a variety of different securities and can encompass many investment strategies and goals.

Some of the most popular and long-running ETFs are built to reflect the performance of key market indexes, thereby giving the investor another index investing option. Other ETFs are crafted to represent an amalgamation of various market interests. You can invest in ETFs comprised of small-cap stocks, mid-cap stocks, large-cap stocks, international stocks, etc. ETFs also allow investors to target specific sectors of the market. There are ETFs that focus on energy, healthcare, commodities, banking, technology, and other industries. These are usually called "sector funds." Some ETFs focus on growth stocks over value stocks and vice versa. There are even ETFs that focus on particular investment tactics, such as writing covered call options (see chapter 6).

Unlike mutual funds, ETFs are not sold to the investor (and bought back) directly by the creators of the fund. They are created and placed on the market by a complex series of transactions. The result is a mutual-fund-like pre-diversified security that can be traded on the market just like a stock. Unlike with mutual funds, ETFs insulate brokerages from the burden of having to hold extra cash to accommodate investors who want to sell back their shares. By virtue of their creation process, ETFs can either be sold to other investors or they can be sold back into the ETF in the form of "creation units." Figure 28 shows how ETFs are created.

The "sponsor," which is the company or financial institution that designs the ETF, is the initiating party. The sponsor will decide what stocks, bonds, or other securities will go into the ETF, how these securities will be selected and proportioned, and what type of market strategy the ETF will represent. Down the road, when the ETF hits the market, the sponsor will need to produce a prospectus for the ETF, similar to those produced for mutual funds. In order to initiate the creation of the ETF, the sponsor submits a plan to the Securities and Exchange Commission (SEC). The SEC's role is to protect the public, so it is more apt to approve the creation of an ETF that is backed by a generally stable and secure assortment of securities.

The Creation of an ETF

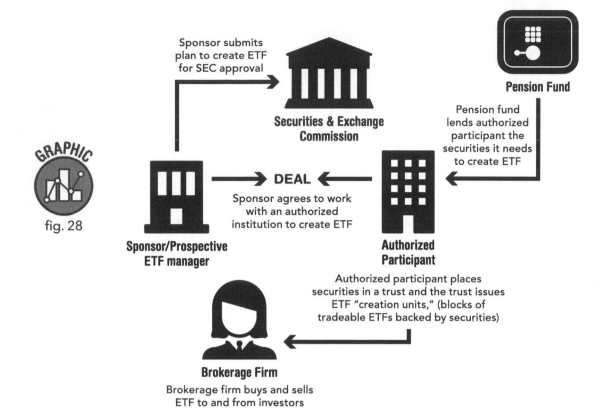

GRAPHIC

fig. 28

Sponsor submits plan to create ETF for SEC approval

Securities & Exchange Commission

Pension Fund

Pension fund lends authorized participant the securities it needs to create ETF

DEAL

Sponsor agrees to work with an authorized institution to create ETF

Sponsor/Prospective ETF manager

Authorized Participant

Authorized participant places securities in a trust and the trust issues ETF "creation units," (blocks of tradeable ETFs backed by securities)

Brokerage Firm

Brokerage firm buys and sells ETF to and from investors

Once the plan is approved, the sponsor will usually partner with a bank or some other large institutional investor to complete the final steps required to bring the ETF to market.

In July of 2013, the Winklevoss twins, best known for their claim to having been the original creators of Facebook, acted as sponsors for the creation of an ETF backed by the crypto-currency Bitcoin. As of October 2016, the SEC was still undecided as to whether it wanted to approve creation of the fund.[24] Were the SEC to approve, the Winklevoss twins, owners of Winklevoss Capital, would not likely try to market their ETF through their own company, but would instead want other parties involved, larger brokerages and market makers.

The role of the authorized participant is to procure the securities needed to create the ETF. Let's say Winklevoss Capital made a deal with Goldman

Sachs, a huge bank with a lot of purchasing power. Goldman Sachs in this case would be acting in the role of the authorized participant. Authorized participants frequently turn to pension funds for the securities needed to create an exchange traded fund. Since pension funds hold assets for long periods, they are often willing to lend out these assets (with interest) for significant lengths of time. The authorized participant then puts these assets in a trust, and the trust in turn issues what are called "ETF creation units," blocks of "stock" that represent the assets held in the trust. Each block represents several thousand shares—50,000 per ETF creation unit is the norm. After all's said and done, what we have is a new enterprise (the trust) that is issuing shares as if it were a publicly traded company. ETFs, technically speaking, are nothing more than legal claims on the contents of the trust. The authorized participant sells ETF shares to investors and other brokers, and the price rises and falls with market demand, hopefully gaining significant value over time. The ongoing function of the trust is to hold the ETF's underlying assets and to cut dividend or interest checks when the trust's assets produce yields.

As a trend, ETF investing has become exceptionally popular in recent years among Gen Xers and Millennials. In 2016, $279 billion in new assets were added to ETFs, bringing the total value of ETF-invested assets to a record high, 2.549 trillion.[25] According to BlackRock Inc., "more Millennials are currently invested in ETFs than investors on average (33 percent vs. 25 percent)."[26] ETFs give younger investors a chance to instantly diversify their holdings while not being subject to the expense and inflexibility of a mutual fund.

On March 10, 2017, the SEC denied the Winklevoss' Bitcoin ETF bid on the grounds that Bitcoin, as an asset, is subject to very little regulation.[27]

ON ETF INVESTING: More and more investor dollars are flowing into ETFs in recent years. Investors are understandably attracted to a pre-diversified security that generally has lower fees and is less actively managed than most mutual funds. I love ETFs, though I do think it is important to note that the prepackaged "trading unit" nature of these stock-like securities may cause them to carry greater risk compared to mutual funds.

Other Funds & Investments

Wall Street, in its own way, is like botanical gardens—rich with complex diversity. That may be stretching it, but there is no denying the persistent creativity and energy of fund managers. Here are a few fund types popular with investors:

Money Market Funds

There are money market mutual funds and money market bank accounts. The latter are offered by banks and credit unions and are usually insured by the FDIC. Money market accounts are similar to standard savings accounts except they usually require higher minimum balances and generate more interest. Money market bank accounts also limit the number of transactions (check writing, withdrawals, etc.) allowed per month.

Money market mutual funds are intentionally configured to remain at one dollar per share. Like money market bank accounts, money market mutual funds are invested in reliable short-term, highly liquid positions, such as short-term bonds and treasuries, the kind of investments that are highly stable but do not generate as much interest as their longer-term equivalents.

Though considered safe investment vehicles, money market funds, unlike most money market accounts, are not FDIC insured. Money market mutual funds are often used by brokerages as "settlement funds" for customers. If a customer of the brokerage sells off a stock, the cash received will automatically go into the money market settlement fund. If a customer adds money to his brokerage account, that money goes straight to the money market settlement account until the customer directs it elsewhere. In this way, within a brokerage account, money market mutual funds essentially act as cash reserves.

A "brokerage account" simply refers to an account opened with a stockbroker or a brokerage firm that can be used to invest in stocks, bonds and other market-based securities.

Some brokerages subcontract with banks to offer customers FDIC insured settlement accounts. If you are curious as to whether your settlement funds are FDIC insured, an examination of your brokerage's account statement or a phone call to your broker should readily clarify the issue.

Relative to other mutual funds, money market funds represent a retreating, minimal-volatility investment position. Though money market funds are not required to be federally insured, they reliably trade at one dollar per share. They are designed to act like cash. As retirement looms near, investors may move more and more of their assets into a money market fund so as to minimize risk and provide a bedrock of retirement funds. Money market funds, like money market accounts, may at times yield higher interest revenues than some savings accounts.

Though rare, it is possible for money market bank accounts and funds to fall short of their one dollar per share value. This phenomenon, colloquially known as "breaking the buck," was witnessed during the 2008 financial crisis following the bankruptcy filings of Lehman Brothers. A money market fund known as the Reserve Primary Fund was forced to lower its value to ninety-seven cents, down from one dollar, after writing off money owed to it by Lehman Brothers. Ninety-seven cents down from a dollar may not seem like a major loss, but because it was in a money market fund, which investors had come to understand was essentially immune from market turmoil, this "breaking of the buck" made major financial news. Though the Reserve Primary Fund was the only money market fund to gain widespread attention at the time, at least twenty-nine others experienced losses severe enough to reduce their value to below the dollar mark.[28] Prior to 2008, no money market fund had broken the buck since 1994, when a small institutional fund had to liquidate at ninety-six cents on the dollar due to bad derivatives investments.[29]

Target Date Funds

Target date funds[a] allow investors to choose a fund tailored to a particular retirement date. Generally, the further away you are from retirement, the more likely your target date fund will favor stocks over bonds. If you are closing in on retirement, then the fund will rely more on bonds and cash positions.

ON TARGET DATE FUNDS: In my opinion, target date funds run a little too conservative across the board. When choosing a target date fund, make sure it adequately corresponds to your risk tolerance; do not just blindly accept it on the grounds that the date on the fund matches your target date for retirement. You may consider investing in funds with target dates that are five to ten years further down the road than your planned retirement date (if you are retiring in 2030, then consider the target date funds for 2035 and 2040), as these funds may offer more aggressive, higher growth investment opportunities.

Hedge Funds

Hedge funds are complicated, relatively expensive, and exclusive. Investors are asked to pay an annual fee for participating in the fund (around 2 percent of the value of their investment). They are also asked to pay out an extra 20 percent of any positive returns. Hedge funds often use a wide variety of investment and risk management tactics, including many high-risk investments that, if successful, will result in big returns for the fund's participants. To participate directly in a hedge fund, you need to be an "accredited investor." The standards required to claim accredited investor status are set forth on a country-by-country basis. In the United States, the SEC is the determining body. Accredited investors in the US must have a net worth of one million dollars or an annual income of at least $200,000 for two years running if single, $300,000 if married. Banks, investment companies, charitable institutions and various other business types may also claim accredited investor status. The supposed logic behind the accredited investor designation is that it is intended to keep certain kinds of investments from the public at large, ensuring that the only investors who participate are competent enough to understand the risks and wealthy enough to endure the potential losses.

Unlike mutual funds, ETFs, and other investment vehicles, hedge funds are not currently regulated by the SEC. In addition to holding the same normal stocks and bonds you would find in an SEC-regulated fund, hedge funds use complex investment tools, such as short selling (selling stock that is not owned and then buying it at a later time). Short selling is only profitable if the stock goes down in value. Hedge funds play both sides of the fence in that way, hence the name "hedge" funds.

Hedge funds also involve the buying and selling of derivatives— these are options and futures contracts, which will be discussed in more detail in chapter 6.

Because of their high risk and uncommon positions, hedge funds are not as liquid as mutual funds—it is often more difficult to get your money out exactly when you want it.

Hedge funds are geared toward an affluent clientele and they conduct their marketing accordingly. Hedge funds also point to their fund manager compensation structure as a selling point. Unlike with mutual fund managers, who take their flat fees regardless of the fund's performance, hedge fund managers' fees are directly linked to fund performance. Though it is a subject of much contention as to whether hedge fund investments outperform the rest of the market,[30] there is no denying that the exclusivity factor, the unique fund manager compensation, and the complex trading methods are enough to get plenty of wealthy investors to buy in.

Annuities

There are many different types of annuities. "Fixed annuities" act essentially like self-commissioned pension plans—you put your money in and the annuity pays you regularly until you die.[b] There is no real investing involved per se in this type of annuity other than you placing your money in the contract and expecting the annuity to produce a cash flow. For retirees, fixed annuities can be attractive because of their perceived simplicity. Complexity abounds, however, within the new generation of annuity products.

There are also "variable annuities," which are more investment-oriented. In a variable annuity, the funds you place into the annuity are invested in the market, usually in the form of sub-accounts that are similar to mutual funds and ETFs. The amount of your annuity payments varies based on the performance of your investments. Variable annuities are controversial in that many believe them to have higher fees, but, you should look at the benefits that come with the higher fees to see if they make sense to purchase. Annuities pay commissions to the insurance brokers who sell them so, as the investor, you should have the broker provide a written statement that states they have no conflicts of interest in selling this kind of investment to you.

NOTE

Annuities are complex financial instruments surrounded by much buzz and controversy. We wanted to at least acknowledge their presence.

Investing in Real Estate

In chapter 1, we introduced the four pillars of investing as defined by investment pro and author Burton Malkiel. We have already covered three pillars fairly extensively—common stocks, bonds, and cash—but we have not yet delved into the world of real estate investing. What many beginner-level investors fail to understand about real estate investing is that it is a lot easier to do than one might think. You do not have to purchase an apartment complex and hire a good property management company in order to make the real estate market work for you. The most common entry point into real estate is by way of a **REIT** (real estate investment trust, pronounced *reet*). REITs pool funds from investors for the purpose of investing in real estate. Like mutual funds and ETFs, REITs can be targeted toward specific real estate sectors. Some REITs specialize in strip mall developments, others in office complexes, others in residential development. REITs may also target geographies all over the world. If you have ever wanted to own condos in suburban Shanghai (and who hasn't?), REITs make it possible.

Some REITs have high liquidity and trade frequently in public markets. At the other end of the spectrum are "non-traded" REITs. Non-traded RE-ITs are still public securities, but investors are generally required to meet certain income and net-worth requirements in order to participate. In my experience, non-traded REITs do not have high yields in the earlier stages of their formation, and the sponsoring REIT company is apt to charge higher fees to account for the high start-up costs that pertain to property acquisition costs and advisor commissions. Eventually, experience tells me, we may expect 5-6% or maybe 7% in dividend yields from more mature non-traded REITs, which means they tend to revert back to the mean of what traded REITs generally offer in their dividend yields (depending on what time of the business cycle they are in). I have also found that publically traded REITs are more transparent and a little easier to understand than their non-traded counterparts with regard to their disclosures to investors. Non-traded REITs usually do not have their value marked each day and their disclosures in my experience can be more opaque and difficult to interpret due to different covenants and rules found in the prospectus. Whether you decide to invest in traded or non-traded REITs, it is important for all REIT investors to read the annual reports for publically traded REITs and the prospectus and related materials for public non-traded REITs in order to make the best investment decisions.

Because REITs are secured with real estate assets, many investors harbor a false impression that they are a rather bland investment and not subject to much volatility. This is actually not the case. Though the real estate market itself is generally less volatile than the stock market, investors' attitudes toward REITs as an investment choice are subject to change. And, as you should know by now, stocks respond to demand. If REITs fall out of favor with investors, then the price of REITs may also fall. In fact, RE-ITs have a funny habit of performing in a wildly different way from other securities. This is why some investors use REITs to offset the volatility in their portfolio. Many times, for instance, when stocks are down across the board, REITs may outperform the broader equity market. In this way

REITs can be exceptionally useful for investors looking to add more lower-correlation securities to their asset mix.

Special Tax Provisions for REITs

REITs have a funny relationship with the IRS. They are required by law to distribute 90 percent of their income to shareholders in the form of dividends. But unlike with most dividend payments, dividends paid by way of REITs are taxed at the investor's standard income tax rate rather than the much lower capital gains rate. On the bright side, REITs are not required to pay corporate income tax, which means that, theoretically, a higher percentage of their earnings will be paid in dividends.[c]

The Tax Factor

When it comes to investment gains, the government is always going to take its cut at some point. But if you are knowledgeable and play within the rules of the tax code, you can minimize your tax liability, especially when pursuing longer-term or retirement investing.

Interest, Dividends, & Capital Gains

If you receive more than ten dollars in interest or dividend payments during the year, you can expect to receive a 1099-INT form (for interest income) or a 1099-DIV form (for dividend income) at tax time. The rates at which you are taxed on these forms of income vary significantly in response to a few key factors. Let's simplify the tax picture by reviewing how a few basic sources of investment income are taxed.

» **Interest income** (income generated by bank accounts, money market accounts, bonds, and loans that you finance): Interest income is taxed at your ordinary income tax rate. All interest income derived from US Treasury and savings bonds are taxed at the federal level only, not the state level. If you have interest income from municipal bonds, then you do not have to pay federal tax on this income, nor do you have to pay state tax on this income if the municipal bonds are issued from a municipality within the state where you reside. If you hold bonds issued outside of your state of residence, then you must pay state tax (to your state of residence) on this interest income.

» **Dividend income** (income generated by stocks and mutual funds containing stocks): Dividend income can be taxed in a few different ways. Like interest income, dividends can be taxed at your normal income tax rate. They can also be taxed as *long-term capital gains*, which is generally preferable for most investors. Dividends taxed as long-term capital gains are known as "qualified dividends." Qualified dividends are taxed at a rate somewhere between 0 percent and 23.8 percent. Unless your annual income is less than $36,000 a year ($72,000 if filing jointly with your spouse) you are going to pay more in taxes on unqualified dividends. In order for dividends to achieve qualified status, the issuing stocks must have been held for a specific period of time (sixty days for common stock and ninety days for preferred stock).

» **Capital gains tax** (income generated by selling a security or other asset at a price higher than the price you paid): If you buy a stock, it goes up in price, and you sell it the next day, then your profit will be taxed as normal income. This is known as a short-term capital gains tax and applies to any profits made from securities held over a period of less than one year. If you hold the security for longer than a year before selling, then any profit you take is considered a long-term capital gain and will be taxed at the lower long-term capital gains tax rate. (Neither dividend income nor capital gains income was affected by the Tax Cuts and Jobs Act of 2017).

Only *realized* short- or long-term gains are taxed, meaning that the investor must have exited the position and taken his profit in cash.

Traditional & Roth IRAs

IRA stands for individual retirement account. Essentially, IRAs are a legal tax shelter for your retirement investments. IRAs can be composed of stocks, bonds, cash, or virtually any other investment type. Traditional IRAs allow retirement planners to contribute pre-tax dollars to their IRA under certain income and eligibility limits. The money put into the IRA each year reduces the contributor's income tax liability for that year. When the contributor begins taking distributions from the IRA, the distributions will be taxed as income at the contributor's current tax rate. If a traditional IRA holder takes distributions before the age of 59½, then in addition to taxes he will be assessed an early withdrawal penalty in the amount of 10 percent of his distribution. The only exceptions to this penalty apply to individuals who incur disabilities and other hardships, and to first-time home buyers, who may withdraw up to $10,000 from their IRA without paying the 10 percent penalty.

The first-time home buyer exemption still requires the payment of taxes on the withdrawn amount. Any person who has not owned a home for the past two years is considered a first-time home buyer.

Roth IRAs can only be opened and contributed to by individuals with a modified adjusted gross income of less than $135,000 annually. Married couples filing jointly must have a modified adjusted gross income of less than $199,000 in order to open or contribute to a Roth IRA.[31] Unlike traditional IRAs, you cannot take your Roth IRA contributions as a tax write-off. What makes Roth IRAs unique, and potentially very lucrative for retirement planners, is that the entirety of your Roth IRA's earnings and contributions can be distributed tax-free after you reach retirement age. This means that you can bypass all income tax associated with the investments you held in your IRA. You can make short-term trades in the market and seize your profits without worrying about tax consequences.

The contributions (not the earnings) you make to a Roth IRA can be withdrawn anytime, free of charge. Once you withdraw more from the Roth IRA than you originally contributed, you are said to be withdrawing earnings. Early withdrawal of the earnings (before age 59½) will result in a 10 percent penalty on the withdrawn amount plus your standard income tax on the earnings portion of your withdrawal. The contributions you have made to your Roth IRA are post-tax income (it has already been taxed). It will not ever be taxed again. But the earnings have not been taxed and will only ever be taxed if you withdraw early.

When you contribute money to a Roth IRA rather than to a traditional IRA, you are contributing taxed income. These contributions will never be taxed again. Your Roth IRA's *earnings*, however, have never been taxed and will never be taxed if you defer your withdrawals until age 59½. If you withdraw your earnings earlier, you will be hit by both the 10 percent penalty *and* the standard income tax liability (on the earnings only).

Like traditional IRAs, Roth IRAs are subject to a special legal provision to assist first-time home buyers. In addition to the penalty-free withdrawal of contributions, first-time home buyers may withdraw up to $10,000 in earnings from their Roth IRAs, penalty-free, to contribute to a down payment on a home. If the Roth IRA has been held for at least five years, then the first-time homeowner's withdrawal will not only be penalty-free, but tax-free as well.

Holding your Roth IRA for at least five years is emphasized again when it comes to retirement distributions. If you decide to start a Roth IRA when you are 58 years old and hope to enjoy tax-free distributions after you turn 59½, a rude surprise awaits. Your earnings will be taxed and you will be subject to the 10 percent penalty. Roth IRAs are subject to the "five year rule," which says that in addition to being 59½, you must have held your Roth IRA for at least five years in order to receive what are known as "qualified" distributions—tax-free, penalty-free.

HANDS-ON LEARNING: I discuss the art of asset allocation, how to use screeners to assist your search for the perfect stock, and go in depth on strategy in my online course. More information and a discount code for the course are available at the front of the book.

Chapter Recap

» An investment return is the percentage gained relative to the original investment amount.

» Asset types (stocks, bonds, mutual funds, ETFs, REITs, etc.) can be strategically allocated in an investment portfolio to lower risk.

» ETFs are pre-diversified securities that can be bought and sold in exchanges, just like stocks.

» Hedge funds are pricey, actively managed funds offered only to high net worth investors.

» Investment earnings (interest, dividends, and capital gains) are taxed at various rates.

» IRAs provide tax advantages for retirement investments.

| 4 |
Decision Time
Deciding When, Where, & How to Invest

Chapter Overview
» Selecting Investments
» Components of Fundamental Analysis

> *Go for a business any idiot can run, because sooner or later, any idiot is probably going to run it.*
>
> – PETER LYNCH

There are a multitude of considerations and viewpoints to take into account when choosing a stock or any kind of investment. The way you choose your investments depends largely on your investment goals, the timeline you are working with, and the level of risk with which you are comfortable. This chapter is devoted to the investment decision making process. We will review the basic ways to judge the quality of various investments via financial statements and other means. We will also review technical and fundamental analysis in this chapter along with some popular investment strategies. But first…

A Bit of Theory, History, & the Lessons of Legends

There is a theory about stock investing that I find thought-provoking. It is known as the *efficient market hypothesis (EMH)*, and it holds that all information about a stock is contained in the stock's price. Regardless of whatever unique knowledge you think you may possess about the stock, EMH holds that the information is already reflected in the stock's current price.

Let's say that MineCorp announces the rollout of a new patented mining drill bit that is going to make coal production dramatically more efficient. Once the announcement about the drill bit hits the press wires, that information will immediately be reflected in the stock price of

MineCorp. The fact that you, a prospective investor in MineCorp, read the story about the new drill bit before you decided to invest gives you no advantage—according to EMH—over the investor who did not read the story but was just looking for a mining stock to buy. The same can be said about the investor who not only read the news about the drill bit, but also rigorously reviewed MineCorp's recent balance sheets and income statements before making up his mind to buy. All the information contained in those financial documents are—according to EMH—already baked into the price, which brings up the question, why even bother with any research at all? Why not just invest in the market, period?

There is no way to prove or disprove the efficient market hypothesis, though there are certainly many ways to criticize it. For starters, a stock's price is based on the abstract concept of demand. No bank, investment firm, or government agency performs rigorous and standardized fundamental and technical analyses of the stock and then dictates its price to the market. Institutions can issue their opinions on various stocks, but at the end of the day, the stock's price is simply a measurement of what investors are willing to pay for future earnings. And the willingness of investors to pay for a stock is not always born of efficiency.

In 2017, the social media, self-styled "photography" company Snapchat issued its initial public offering (IPO). As with many IPOs, Snapchat came charging out of the gates as the hype behind the stock drove the price up. Meanwhile, as with most IPOs, shareholders within the company were subject to a contractual "lock-up period." They were unable to sell any of the stock that they owned until after a period of time (denoted by a contract) expired. Lock-up periods are intended to prevent company insiders from flooding the market with shares and driving the stock price down. On July 31st, 2017, SNAP's lockup period expired and the stock plunged by a whopping 5% as company insiders cashed out. The added trading volume coupled with the perception of flagging confidence sufficiently depressed demand for the stock. SNAP Shares, at least for a short period of time, appeared to be less valuable than they actually were. Later that day, SNAP rebounded, recovering its "normal" value.

These complicating factors that attend to the release of an IPO are an example of how the stock's price is at times walled off from critical dimensions of the stock's value, a direct challenge to the efficient market hypothesis.

A company's owners, senior officers, or even employees, if judged to have material, non-public information about the company, are not allowed to sell their shares, even after the lock-up period expires, as this would be considered "insider trading." These so-called "company insiders" *can* sell, however, if the basis for their sale is not specifically tied to the information they are privy to, or if the info they are privy to has already been made public.

Another major price distortion results when the price of a sector or the price of the market as a whole begins to swell for no good reason. This is known as a "bubble" and is the result of a kind of mob mentality, whereby investors irrationally bid up prices to unjustifiable heights. During the mid-aughts, 2005–2007, countless investors were "getting rich" due to the rapid appreciation of real estate. Just like the tech boom in the late 1990s, investors saw their friends and neighbors making quick fortunes and did not want to be left out, so they piled on. The demand for the assets continued to raise the price, confirming (seemingly) the inevitability of the upward trend. More investors piled on late, hoping to catch the train before it ran out of gas. But not only did it run out of gas, it crashed spectacularly.

The 2008 financial collapse, aka the Great Recession, was linked to this real estate bubble. Mortgage-backed securities (investments that depended on the reliable payment of mortgage debt) were brought to the market in droves. Their high quality ratings (often BBB or better) belied the fact that they had toxic assets rolled into them (mortgages issued to home buyers who had a high chance of defaulting). These flawed securities were then bundled into funds alongside hundreds of other mortgage-backed securities. According to their prospectuses, these funds were investment grade with high credit ratings, not likely to fail—safe investments.

NOTE

The structural causes of the Great Recession extend well beyond Wall Street recklessness and the weak government oversight of the time. It was nearly a decade prior to the collapse that President Bill Clinton, in an effort to expand homeownership, inadvertently helped lay the groundwork for the collapse by enacting policies encouraging banks to issue "subprime" loans.[32]

In his book *The Random Walk Guide to Investing*, Burton G. Malkiel offers amusing accounts of speculative investment bubbles throughout history. In one such account, Malkiel cites the example from 1711 of a company called the South Sea Company. In a rather corrupt exchange, the government of England gave the South Sea Company a monopoly over trade routes to South America. Investors lined up by the droves and the company's stock shot up. The price of the stock was climbing at such a fast pace that investors could buy stock one day and sell their stock a few days later for a huge profit. The allure of this skyrocketing security set off a general investing trend in England, and new investment "opportunities" began to come out of the woodwork. Many of these opportunities were pure gimmick and nonsense, but the demand for investment opportunities was so high that people did not require rock solid reports, plans, or even a compelling story. They were looking for any reason to give their money away. One company focused on importing donkeys from Spain, despite England's more than abundant domestic supply. Another company claimed it would revolutionize warfare through the creation of a machine gun that shot different kinds of bullets based on the religious affiliation of the target. And one idea, perhaps the most ambitious and ridiculous of them all, solicited large investments for "a company carrying on an undertaking of great advantage, but nobody to know what it is."

Those who believe in research, sobriety, and the value of financial analysis of investments would undoubtedly point to the many market bubbles as evidence that the efficient market hypothesis is at least partially flawed. Even so, the current market price of a stock or other security should not go underappreciated. There are millions and millions of investors out there shaping the demand for stocks through various approaches to valuation. The market as a whole knows a lot more than you do about most things. Just remember that masses of people can act irrationally, even insanely.

> *I can calculate the motions of heavenly bodies, but not the madness of people.*[33]
> – **SIR ISAAC NEWTON** (one of the big losers in the South Sea Company bubble)

In his book *The Forever Portfolio*, author/investor James Altucher offers readers his advice for choosing solid long-term stocks. As with many talented traders, Altucher has a knack for seeing what is right in front of his (and everyone else's) face. Among other tips, he urges investors to pick the less flashy stocks, the ones that do not make regular appearances on the financial talk shows.[34] This might seem like a rather simplistic approach to choosing stocks (and it is) but the deeper lesson here is that investors should remain conscious of the forces that create demand and confidence. Apple Inc. is by no means a bad investment, but it is such a well-known stock and trades in such high volumes that there may be a persistent inflation of demand coming from market newcomers and others. Altucher recommends looking for steals in the dusty, less sexy corners of the marketplace. Consider, for instance, the Canadian auto parts supplier Magna International. It is a rather boring company that produces replacement parts for automobiles. Nevertheless, it is a steadily growing, solid stock (its investors got a return of 33.5 percent last year and 102 percent over the last five years).

Altucher does not mention Magna specifically, but he does bring up the Barnes Group, which makes parts for airplane engines and railroads. Barnes is another stock that, although not likely to generate a lot of fuss, has a history of quietly turning profits for investors. And sure enough, the Barnes Group has returned over 100 percent of its value back to investors since Altucher published *The Forever Portfolio* in 2008.[35]

Altucher's paean to "boring" stocks is not meant to imply that you should not invest in a stock just because it is well-known or popular. However, if you are particularly interested in owning shares of a certain company—perhaps it is a company with which you are familiar, whose products you enjoy—consider investing! Why not? If you are a genuine fan, then you may be more inclined to enjoy your research and due diligence. Should you decide to buy, then you will enjoy keeping up with the latest news. You may even get involved in shareholder voting. Famed investor and former fund manager Peter Lynch says, "Know what you own and why you own it." Lynch is notorious for his strange but possibly brilliant habit of watching women shop and observing their reactions to various products and retail venues. Perhaps it was due in part to his observant nature that Lynch was buying up shares in Hanesbrands Inc., Dunkin Donuts, and Wal-Mart long before the brands caught on.

Investing legend Warren Buffett urges investors to only involve themselves with stocks if they are ready to commit for the long haul. "If you aren't willing to own a stock for ten years, don't even think about owning it for ten minutes." Buffett also echoes Lynch (or perhaps Lynch echoes Buffett) in his reluctance to invest in companies or industries he does not understand. Buffett, for instance, claims he does not understand the intricacies of tech stocks. Hence you will notice that tech stocks are conspicuously underrepresented in his firm's portfolio.[36] James Altucher—who, in addition to writing *The Forever Portfolio*, also authored *Trade Like Warren Buffett*—appears to draw much of his investing philosophy from Buffett, particularly when it comes to maintaining a disciplined, long-term focus. Altucher quotes Buffett as saying, "If a company is going to be here twenty years from now, then it is probably a good buy right now."[37]

Sir John Templeton is another highly respected investor, renowned for his uncanny ability to buy low and sell high. The concept of buying into weakness and selling into strength that I often emphasize with my clients can be traced to Templeton. He was continuously attracted to companies and countries that were, as he described, "at points of maximum pessimism." Among other examples of remarkable foresight, Templeton was one of the first to invest in postwar Japan, and was also one of the first to sell off his Japanese investments in the mid-'80s, right before Japan's economic collapse.[38]

Another one of my favorites is Jeremy Siegel, Professor of Finance at the Wharton School and author of the highly acclaimed *Stocks for the Long Run*. He is also quite poignant in identifying and holding a spotlight on the most common and disastrous mistakes that many investors make. According to Siegel, "Fear has a far greater grasp on human action than the impressive weight of historical evidence."

How to Choose a Stock, ETF, or Other Security

The stock selection process for many longer-term investors is often quite simple. It involves first having some level of personal familiarity with the company or industry—maybe you are a customer, or the stock was recommended by a friend, or you heard about it on television. Once your interest is piqued, take a look at a few historical charts, maybe a quick glance over some of the financial metrics, the P/E ratio, the dividend yield. Next, ask yourself if this company is going to last; is it poised to service a persistent and growing need in the marketplace? Can you see yourself owning this same stock in twenty years' time?

The narrative element—the story you tell yourself about the stock or other security under consideration—can be formed in a variety of ways. Even though you may be looking to invest in a company that, as Warren Buffett says, will still be around twenty years down the road, neither you, nor Warren, nor anyone can predict the future. Good companies can fail. Even Buffett himself, though he initially sets out to own a stock for twenty years or more, does not always make the right call and finds himself selling off stocks earlier than he had planned in order to contain a loss. We will talk more about monitoring the health of your portfolio later in this chapter. Right now, I would like you to think about how you are going to choose your initial investments—your entry-points into the market.

Long-term investment pros like Buffett and Altucher are big fans of identifying persistent macro-level market trends and the companies that benefit from them. In *The Forever Portfolio*, Altucher cites the threat of global pandemic, the need for clean water, computer virus protection, and even tattoo removal as examples of market forces likely to endure throughout the decades. He refers to these forces as "tidal-wave-like demographic forces." Altucher's strategy is to identify and invest in baskets of companies positioned to capitalize on these trends, giving heavier weight (more investment dollars) to the companies with stronger balance sheets.[39]

I might add to Altucher's analysis that there are certain market phenomena just as prevalent as and even more fundamental than the "tidal-wave-like demographics" he identifies. The vast majority of the global food supply, for instance, is manufactured and distributed by only about a dozen or so companies, most of them publicly traded. This small group of companies owns hundreds of everyday household brands.[40] Given the sweeping command these companies exert over an industry as fundamental as consumer foods, it is no surprise that Warren Buffett has "pulverized the food industry market" with serial acquisitions (no pun intended) in this space.[41]

Here is the thing to keep in mind regardless of which sector you decide to invest in or what strategies or advice you take to heart: it is easy to pick a few winning stocks, especially when the market as a whole is performing well. The mark of an excellent investor is the ability to consistently *outperform* the market. Such is the constant, obsessive objective of Buffett, Templeton, Lynch and all the other investment giants. Outperforming the market is also the mandate of all the "genius" hedge fund and mutual fund managers. Think about it—if investors are paying significant sums to a fund manager, then they are going to expect bigger returns than what they would have gained by placing their assets in a simple index fund. It's all about beating the market.

Now, before we get into the trenches and talk about how to beat the market, it is important to note that there is absolutely nothing wrong with a beginner-level investor making a gut-hunch stock pick, investing a reasonable amount of money, following the stock for a while and seeing how it goes. Doing so will allow new investors to follow and learn about the behavior of the market and to gauge their tolerance for risk and market volatility. If the market is bullish, there is likely more to gain than there is to lose. Go ahead and invest in your favorite company and get your feet wet.

Use Stock Screeners to Search Out the Right Picks

Over time, your pre-investment research should become more exacting and complex. As you gain in proficiency, you should strive to build a portfolio that outperforms the indexes that best reflect your holdings. If you are concentrated in small-cap companies, for instance, then you will want to evaluate your performance alongside the Russell 2000 index. If you are more of a large-cap investor, then you will look to the S&P 500 as a reference point. One of the first realizations made by investors on their way to becoming highly competent is that there exists a wide universe of stocks and other securities out there of which you have no personal knowledge. Many of these stocks will quietly outperform the market, generating fantastic returns for those few fortunate enough to take note of them.

One highly efficient way of getting lesser-known but promising stocks to appear on your radar is through the use of a stock screener. These tools are offered by brokerages and other companies, sometimes for free and sometimes for a price. Screeners allow investors to filter their view of various stocks.

You want to look at energy sector stocks that have a P/E ratio of less than 17. Your screening application will return a list of stocks for you to choose from that meets these qualifications.

You can screen for debt levels, growth trends, earnings per share, dividend yield, and a variety of other metrics. You can also use screeners to help you better summarize the historical behavior of stocks.

You want to buy a stock that has historically outperformed its expected quarterly earnings, then you can instruct your screener to identify these particular stocks.

When a stock outperforms or underperforms its expected quarterly or annual earnings forecasts, it is known as a positive or negative "earnings surprise."

As a CFP® practitioner, I occasionally use screeners to identify stocks and REITs that have higher yields. My objective in most cases is to build a securities portfolio for a client that will produce enough yield income to forestall any need for selling off shares in the principal investments. After enough high yield securities are identified and purchased, we can bring a client's portfolio to a "critical mass" at which the yield income is sufficient to meet the client's day-to-day living needs. These high yield securities may also make great alternatives to bonds, which don't always offer robust returns, and, unlike stocks, do not readily appreciate in value during a bull market. Depending on your risk tolerance, stocks that pay good dividends may make a good substitute for bonds.

The Eternal Investing Conundrum & General Market Forces

If you are going to invest, prepare to be a little frustrated at times. You will be forced to watch as a stock that you recently sold soars to new heights. And you will be forced to watch what you thought was a rock solid investment plummet in value. To make matters more frustrating, in many of these cases you will be able to reasonably explain why the stock behaved the way it did, but only after the fact.

There is a phenomenon of investing that I like to call "the eternal investing conundrum." And this phenomenon lends itself too well to a sports analogy for me to pass on the opportunity. Before a match-up in any sport, where two teams or individuals of reasonably similar talents are slated to go head-to-head in competition, it is impossible to predict who will come out on top. However, after it is all said and done and one or the other team has emerged victorious, it is usually not at all difficult to explain *why* one team won and the other lost. The stock market operates in exactly the same way. Consider the predicaments of GM and Ford during the 2008 financial crisis. The conventional wisdom seemed to be that because of its superior size, GM would be in a better position than Ford to weather the impact of the crisis on the auto industry. But at the end of the day it was GM, not Ford, that required a taxpayer bailout. Ford actually did quite well throughout that time, comparatively speaking. With the advantage of hindsight, we can explain why GM found itself in such a precarious position. The combination of its pension and debt obligations put strain on its cash reserves. The company was headed toward the abyss. Without a bailout, GM would have been unable to pay its employees and suppliers within a few weeks' time.[42] It is impossible to reliably predict who is going to win and by how much, but when we are aided by the power of hindsight, we can offer fairly airtight explanations as to why a stock survived, soared, or collapsed.

Despite the value of hindsight, it is quite possible for investors to become overly reliant on (or dogmatic about) past trends. As Jeremy Siegel says, "Hindsight plays tricks on our minds."

In theory, acquiring a greater understanding of these factors will add to our wisdom and lead to better decision making.

As we strive to compile the many, many lessons that have been taught and retaught by the market, let's begin first with a rundown of macro-level factors or general market forces that affect the market as a whole.

» **Interest rates** – When the US Federal Reserve lowers interest rates, the economy should respond favorably, adding jobs and increasing the circulation of capital. Lower interest rates mean that capital comes cheaper. It also creates an environment where loans are not as lucrative for the lender. This gives investors more incentive to put their money in stocks rather than to loan it out or leave it in the bank. By contrast, when interest rates are high, investors are more likely to leave their money in the bank and collect a decent return without having to endure the risks inherent in the stock market.

» **Political stability** – Wall Street is neither Democrat nor Republican turf. The primary concern on Wall Street is making money. The only time politics really weighs in is when a political crisis or uncertainty about various policies, elections, or international events makes investors nervous. Nervous investors do not invest in stocks but instead lock their money away until conditions stabilize.

» **Employment** – High employment rates are a sign that businesses are confident and are pursuing expansion. Low employment is a sign that businesses are not hitting their targets and need to cut costs. Investors are generally much more interested in buying stock during periods of high employment, hence the demand for and prices of stocks usually flow in direct proportion to the employment rate.

» **Taxes** – The promise of lower taxes should provide an across-the-board boost for the market, whereas the promise of higher taxes can be disquieting for businesses and drive stock prices down.

» **Economy** – The economy is subject to a persistent ebb and flow of business activity known as the "business cycle." Often measured by GDP (gross domestic product) the business cycle expands and recedes in conjunction with periods of economic growth and decline. An economy in recession is marked by lower interest rates, outflow of investment from individual stocks and stock mutual funds, and more reliance on cash and short-term bonds. An expanding economy is marked by rising interest rates and more investment in stock mutual funds and in individual stocks.

fig. 29

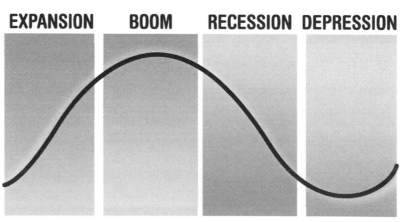

A Simple Rendering of the Standard Business Cycle

As Sir John Templeton would say, the best time to invest in stocks and mutual funds is "at points of maximum pessimism." Mutual funds that hold stocks report their net outflows (dollars divested from the fund). You can use this and other data to gauge when investors are most pessimistic.

Another useful market barometer is the yield offered on current treasury notes, particularly the ten-year treasury note. As was discussed in chapter 1, when the interest rate on the ten-year is high, it is a sign of a competitive market, since the T-note is forced to offer a high rate just to attract buyers away from stocks. When the yield is lower it is a sign that there are enough interested buyers to bid down the rate. The note can offer a lower rate and still compete in the market, as investors would rather put money in bonds than in stocks.

In an ideal world, you would be holding more bonds and cash and fewer stocks when the economy takes a turn for the worse. In this way you would be preserving and safeguarding your principal investment. Conversely, when the economy is performing well, it would be great to find more stocks and fewer bonds in your portfolio, as you would be the beneficiary of more aggressive growth. Unfortunately, since we are unable to predict the future, we will not always have the perfectly configured portfolio for every occasion. This is why it is important to establish a personal investing plan—a set of parameters and asset allocation targets that help you limit your risk and maximize your potential for gains. Part of your plan might include selling some of your stocks and buying more bonds when the market goes up by a certain percentage. Reflexively, you might plan to purchase more stocks and divest yourself of more bonds after the market declines by a certain percentage. The parameters you define should take into account several different factors. For instance, if the market is emerging out of a recession and poised to grow steadily for a long period of time, then you may want to loosen up your parameters drastically and hold on to your stocks as the market regains its strength. Alternatively, if the market is peaking, hitting record highs, and there has not been a bear market for a long while, then it may be time to tighten up your parameters and be more willing to sell out of stocks and buy into bonds.

Market Strategies: How to Win in Good Times & in Bad

Some investors attempt to "time the market." They try to predict when the next crash is coming and then they sell all of their stock, so as to rescue their investment gains from the crash they are predicting. Some of them even go so far as to place their money in "bear funds," which are specifically designed to prosper in a down market. Timing the market, however, is an incredibly difficult feat to accomplish and is discouraged by investment professionals. To be successful in timing the market you have to be right two times. First, you have to guess the top of the market and sell off your investments while prices are highest. Next, you have to guess the bottom of the market and reinvest while prices are at a low point. If you are wrong in either phase of your market timing strategy, then not only do you suffer a waste in trading expense, but you also face meaningful losses in the form of opportunity cost. Historically, the brunt of market gains is concentrated into a few high-performing days throughout the year. When you take all of your money out in an attempt to avoid a down period, you risk incurring serious losses in the form of a missed rally.

While only about 1 percent of your portfolio return comes from successful timing of the market, about 93 percent of returns come from diligent asset allocation—continually maintaining a well-proportioned mix of various asset types in order to strike a sensible risk/reward balance.[43] If you are mindful of your asset allocation and consistently rebalance your portfolio when needed, you will improve your likelihood of buying low and selling high. You will also lower your risk and keep your exposure to important sectors (such as international and emerging markets) consistent.

You may find yourself with a stock-heavy portfolio when the market goes down. When this happens, resist the urge to sell. Stocks do rebound. If you panic and sell, then you are likely going to take losses that you do not have to take and perhaps irreversibly damage your opportunity to realize your retirement goals. This sad phenomenon was something I witnessed firsthand in my early career while working for a discount brokerage. I saw countless investors selling prolifically into down markets, usually out of a panicked notion that the markets were doomed to never recover. A much better strategy is to buy when the market is down, because many stocks affected by a general downturn are likely to recover their value and return a healthy profit.

Bear markets are inherently temporary. Our economy has a 100 percent track record of recovery following recessions.

You may also use dividend earnings to help you rebalance your portfolio. Your brokerage account will likely give you the option of having your dividends automatically reinvested into the stocks and funds that generated them. As a CFP® practitioner, my approach is a little different. As a matter of best practice, rather than automatically reinvesting dividend yields and capital gains, I often move this income into my clients' settlement accounts, so as to build up a strong cash position. Once a certain level of cash is available in the settlement account, we take a look across the portfolio and identify areas that have not performed as well as others. That is where we reinvest. By bolstering the portfolio's underperforming segments, we end up getting more shares for less money. Over time, this approach may generate a great deal of value for the client.

While you cannot control or always predict the behavior of securities on the market, you can control your portfolio diversification strategy. Let's take a look at a few other areas of diversification that should be considered when selecting stocks and other securities.

Emerging Markets

Investors may consider devoting a portion of their portfolios to emerging markets. Thirty years ago it was primarily advanced economies that were responsible for the bulk of global production. But with the onset of globalization and the reduction of trade barriers, more and more production is coming out of emerging markets, close to 50 percent of the world's GDP, in fact.[44] An emerging market is one that is fast becoming a developed market. Examples would include Brazil, Mexico, China, and Vietnam. While concerns about political stability, growing protectionist/isolationist political movements, and sustainable modernization may sway some investors, if you have room for risk in your portfolio and if you have time on your side, then you may seriously consider getting into some emerging market funds.

If you are in your sixties and eyeing retirement, then you should be considerably more cautious about investing in emerging markets. Though the returns on these securities have recently been remarkable, the longer-term picture remains subject to volatility.

ON EMERGING MARKETS & AGGRESSIVE INVESTING IN GENERAL: I like to think of emerging market investments the way I think about investments in small companies. There is a lot of growth potential. Just be sure to diversify, as emerging markets have a tendency to swing mightily, tempest-like, from year to year.

One year your basket of emerging market stocks may earn an average return of 80 percent. The next year they may be down by 60 percent or more.

International Investing

In addition to investing in emerging markets, general international investing is used by many investors as a way to offset the risk of an across-the-board downturn in domestic stocks. International investing also offers a unique potential investment reward. In addition to the standard rewards of capital gains and dividend payments, international investing can produce returns in the form of currency rises against the dollar. If you invest in a mining company in Canada (a country known for its promising mining stocks) and the Canadian dollar (the "loonie") spikes in value relative to the dollar, then your investment is automatically worth more. If you sell the stock, you will get more US dollars per share.

As you may have gathered, the fluctuation in currency values also adds a unique risk opportunity. If the country where you have your international investment suffers a currency collapse, then your return in US dollars will automatically sink. However, if the company is a solid one, the currency collapse may provide an opportunity to buy more shares at a lower price. Not only are your international investments affected by the value of the host country's currency value, they are also affected by the interest rate changes, political climate, and tax laws of the host country. When you invest internationally you are subject to *foreign tax withholding*. Foreign tax withholdings are levied against capital gains, interest payments, and dividends paid to foreigners.

We make an investment in a Chinese company and that company wants to pay us $100 in dividends. We will only receive $90 of that payment due to China's 10 percent foreign withholding rate on dividends. China also withholds 10 percent on interest payments made to foreign investors and 30 percent on capital gains realized by foreign investors.

The good news for US investors is that the IRS has rules in place to prevent your earnings from being taxed twice. Income generated through foreign investments and taxed by foreign governments can often be sheltered from US tax by way of foreign tax credits and itemized deductions. It is up to the IRS and the federal government to decide which foreign investments are eligible for these tax protections. Income from countries with hostile or poor relations with the United States will not be subject to tax protections.

Investors using tax advantaged brokerage accounts, such as IRAs, have to pay special attention to international investments. There is no way to issue foreign tax credits to these investors, because they are not paying any domestic tax on their investment income. Therefore, when foreign governments tax their investment income, there is no way to recover these expenses. This is a difficult conundrum for retirement investors, as international investments and emerging market investments in particular can play a key role in an appropriately diversified and growth-oriented portfolio. You need international investment, but you do not want to sacrifice substantial earnings to unrecoverable foreign taxes. One solution is to make the majority of your international investments in countries like the United Arab Emirates, Sweden, the Netherlands, Latvia, and Estonia, where no tax is withheld from foreign investment revenues. Check with your brokerage for an exhaustive, country-by-country listing of foreign investment tax levels. Another approach is to concentrate your foreign investment in ETFs and mutual funds. The underlying investments that form these securities are preselected or actively managed by analysts intent on maximizing returns. While ETFs and mutual funds will not free you of your tax obligations, they do offer a simplified approach to acquiring much-needed international exposure for your portfolio.

The Three Biggest Mistakes Investors Make

Over the course of my career I have watched a lot of investors make mistakes. Believe it or not, I have even made a few of my own. Here are a few mistakes that I see time and again:

1. **Investing too conservatively** – Just because we are nearing retirement does not mean we should dramatically alter our investment strategy. We could very well still be alive twenty, thirty, or forty years after our retirement date; we will need our investments to continue to grow and to keep up with the pace of inflation.

2. **Beginning too late** – As discussed previously in this book (though we really cannot emphasize it enough): your money goes further the earlier you invest it.

3. **Not investing enough** – Your investment contributions should be a fixed expense in your monthly budget.

Investor Returns vs. Investment Returns

Recent studies show that, left to their own devices, most investors consistently underperform the markets.[45] This phenomenon is sometimes referred to as "investor vs. investment returns." The "investor" is the human actor, who is subject to panic selling, thinks past performance is a good indicator of future performance, attempts to time the market, and suffers from a range of other money-destroying compulsions and illusions that give way to bad investment behavior.

The "investment" component refers to the market itself, which of course is not subject to forming bad habits of its own accord and simply returns what it returns. The bottom line is that investments outperform investors.

In addition to being a fine advertisement for the value of a good financial advisor, the investor vs. investment phenomenon also illustrates the very real challenge of maintaining investment discipline. You may feel quite comfortable with many of the investment techniques and strategies discussed in this book thus far, but when faced with the prospect of putting these ideas into consistent practice, you may find that responding to the market in the right way and on a consistent basis is not as easy as you think. We will dive deeper into the psychology of investing in chapter 7.

ON INVESTOR VS. INVESTMENT RETURNS: *Time in* the market is about a hundred times more valuable than *timing* the market. Let the market do the work and don't get in your own way.

Paying Attention to Your Investments

There is a key difference between "investing" and "trading." If you are investing, then you are thinking long term. You have specific financial goals in mind, such as retiring or buying a new home. When you are trading, you are attempting to act with scant knowledge about the market, having seen what you believe others have failed to see. You make transactions and turn profits (or suffer losses) in short succession, getting in and getting out, often within the same day. Trading has more of a speculative connotation, whereas investing usually implies a more thorough binding of the investor's interests with the interests of the company. Traders, by contrast, often buy and sell stocks in companies while knowing very little, if anything, about the company's principal business, much less the quality of its balance sheets. A trader is purely interested in predicting the short-term movement of a stock's price. Not to say that an investor never trades. He does, but usually within the context of maintaining a target asset allocation or in response to major macroeconomic shifts. The investor's default approach is to buy and to hold, often as long as possible.

The financial journeys of investor and trader follow markedly different paths. Both are subject to turbulence and uncertainty, but much more so in the case of the trader.

fig. 30

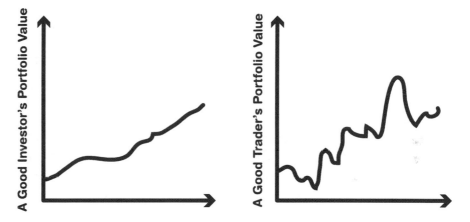

The graph above displays the comparative volatility of portfolio value (investor vs. trader) during a bull market

We will discuss the concerns of the "trader" in more depth later in this chapter and in chapter 6. For the "investor," constant portfolio monitoring is a thankless task. If you become hung up on the small day-to-day or even month-to-month movements of the market, then you are not really accomplishing much other than distracting yourself with noise. If you have an impulsive personality, especially if you cannot stand losing money, then you are likely to do more harm than good. A down day in the market might spook you into prematurely selling off investments that are meant to be long-term positions. Stocks will rise and fall, sometimes dramatically in one direction or another, in a mostly meaningless flurry of activity. A perfectly competent investor needs only look at her portfolio's performance a couple of times a year. This is the time to check on the recent performance of your investments and to consider rebalancing.

You have an investment (let's say in a drug company) that skyrockets and becomes so valuable it now accounts for 50 percent of your entire portfolio value. The smart play would be to sell off some shares and reinvest in other sectors and other asset classes. In this way you secure your portfolio

from massive losses in the event your high performer gets brought back down to earth. What you have essentially done is incorporate the drug company's outstanding performance back into a well-balanced (and now higher-value) portfolio.

You do not need to rebalance your portfolio every day. Once a year is usually fine, so long as there is no severe deterioration in the economy. In the event of such a downturn, you should consider not only rebalancing as soon as you can, but also reallocating your investments toward assets more appropriate for a down economy. If the economy is roaring, then you might consider selling off some of your best-performing stocks or mutual funds and using the profits to shore up the investment areas in your portfolio that have not performed as well.

Some investors are overly attentive to their investments, checking their stocks several times a day so they will be privy to the latest up- or down-tick. If you are unable to extract yourself from the day-to-day performance of your investments, that is fine, but do not expect your over-attentiveness to be rewarded by higher than average returns. Unless you are a highly skilled trader (not an investor), the minute-by-minute movement of stocks or other securities contains very little if any relevant information. And most importantly, don't panic and rush to sell when the market goes down. Being forced to watch yourself lose money from time to time is the price you pay for your front-row seat.

As futile as it can be, if you are intent on monitoring your portfolio like a hawk, then you should always be scouting out new securities. Don't make a habit of regularly selling off your current positions in order to jump on the next great opportunity that you come across, but do keep an investment wish list and use it to motivate yourself to make ongoing contributions to your brokerage account. Especially true for long-term savers: making regular out-of-pocket contributions to your investment accounts is one of the most critical and foolproof investment strategies one can adopt.

Fundamental & Technical Analysis of a Stock

There is a concept in investing called *due diligence*. In the world of securities, the idea of due diligence came to popularity when the government mandated certain disclosure standards for brokerages selling securities. It was mandated by the Securities Act of 1933 that a brokerage had to obtain (through due diligence) and disclose specific information about securities before they could be sold to the general public. The legal requirement of brokers to carry out due diligence ensured that phony companies could not come out of the woodwork and bring bogus or distorted securities to market through a broker without the broker being directly responsible. According to the 1933 law, brokers who do not conduct due diligence on the securities they sell or do not disclose these findings to the customer are liable for losses incurred by the customer.

Another round of due diligence, though not legally required, should be carried out by the purchaser of a security—you. When deciding on the purchase of a stock or other security, it behooves the buyer to rigorously investigate the integrity of the underlying asset. In the case of a stock, the underlying asset is the company which is issuing the equity. *Fundamental analysis* can be defined as the evaluation of core quantitative and qualitative attributes defining the financial vitality of a security's underlying assets. *Technical analysis* can be defined as looking for patterns and trends in a stock price over selected periods.

The language of the technical analyst includes phrases such as, "the stock is leveling off," or "the stock has hit a ceiling." Technical analysis relies on charts, graphs, figures, trends, trading volume, and perception, whereas fundamental analysis is more concerned with financials—looking squarely and objectively at the healthiness of the business or other underlying asset.

Traders, as opposed to investors, are more likely to rely on technical rather than fundamental analysis. It does not matter to a trader whether a company's stock price is warranted or sustainable, what matters is whether the trader can accurately predict whether the stock price will move up or down during the course of a couple of days or a few hours. Good technical analysts are students of history. They watch for spikes in trading volume, indicating investment by a large institutional investor, and they know how the stock price is likely to respond in the wake of such an investment. They know how to pick out where a stock is due to rebound after a market correction causes its price to temporarily dip.

Despite the value of good technical analysis, fundamental analysis is less abstract and may be easier to master. Furthermore, the investing approach is considerably less expensive than the trading approach.

More trades means more overhead in the form of brokerage fees.

We will revisit trading and technical analysis again in chapter 5, but for now, let's take a look at the basics of investing by way of fundamental analysis.

Corporate Governance

Corporate governance refers to the functioning of a company's management apparatus. The structure of a corporation usually includes an executive team, comprised of a CEO/president, various vice presidents, chief operations officers (COOs), chief financial officers (CFOs), chief information officers (CIOs), and other top-level (C-level) executives. These managers are employees of the company and are overseen by the company's board of directors. The board usually has the power to establish policies that the management must abide by. Board members are usually elected by the company's stockholders.

When assessing a company's corporate governance as part of your fundamental analysis, look for a qualified board of directors. Membership should include business leaders that bring valuable insight and experience to the table. The board's policies should emphasize transparency, accountability, and a commitment to serving the interest of the company's shareholders. The company's goals should be well-defined, appropriate for the industry, and reflective of the company's optimal capabilities. Each goal should be accompanied by a practical, well-thought-out strategy with a clear emphasis on tracking results.

Problems in corporate governance can be difficult to detect and often do not come to light until after a crisis has transpired, and usually by that time the company's stock price has already been forced down. Poor transparency, accounting and reporting inaccuracies, non-active board members, and poor executive leadership may all contribute to problematic and potentially value-crushing corporate governance.

10-Ks, 10-Qs, and Balance Sheets

When you invest in a publicly traded company, you will have access to that company's key financial reports, such as balance sheets, income statements, and cash flow statements. A fundamental analysis of a company involves reviewing these documents and assessing the company's overall vitality. Companies are required to issue comprehensive annual financial reports called *10-Ks* that are supplemented quarterly by *10-Qs*. These reports are clear and to the point and contain objective, straightforward data about the company's performance.

There is no singular standard for a good financial statement. The best way to learn is to study, compare, and contrast multiple statements of similarly sized companies in the same sector over the same period of time. Financials from different sectors, such as tech, retail, and healthcare, behave in different ways, and using financial reports to understand what makes these industries tick is going to be a work in progress. When you first begin conducting fundamental analysis or technical analysis it can help to limit yourself to a particular market sector in which you have interest. Study as many companies in this sector as you can. Read articles and analyst reports. Consider investing in a subscription to a research publication like Value Line,[46] which will provide you with robust reporting and analyst commentary on any number of securities. Look for patterns of steadily increasing revenue (sales) and increasing earnings (profit).

Take note also of the company's **debt-to-asset ratio** or debt ratio. Debt is a ubiquitous phenomenon in business. Some industries, such as utilities and mining, are likely to have higher debt because they are capital-intensive. Equipment and real estate costs in these industries can be extremely pricey and are often financed by debt. Other sectors, such as the technology sector, are not nearly so capital-intensive, and, as a result, companies in this sector have lower debt. The closer a company is to a debt-to-asset ratio of 100 percent, the closer it is to being in the precarious position of having more debt than assets. Debt in certain situations can be a headwind that slows down a company's revenue and earnings streams. In other situations debt can be a tailwind, as when a company that has debt has access to capital, which allows it to do things like launch a sales campaign, invest in advertising, or buy real estate.

Another way to measure debt is by using a **debt-to-equity** ratio, which measures the amount of debt a company holds in relation to the total value of its outstanding shares. We can use information provided on financial statements to calculate various ratios, such as debt-to-asset and debt-to-equity. Let's take a look at last year's balance sheet for a fictitious company called WidgetCorp (WDGT).

A balance sheet will always have information on assets, liabilities, and equity. Figure 31 includes only assets and liabilities. We will review the equity portion of the balance sheet when we calculate debt-to-equity ratio.

In Millions of USD (except for per share items)	
Cash & Equivalents	1,011.32
Short Term Investments	3,753.74
Cash and Short Term Investments	4,765.06
Accounts Receivable - Trade, Net	833.03
Receivables - Other	-
Total Receivables, Net	833.03
Total Inventory	-
Prepaid Expenses	194.21
Other Current Assets, Total	47.47
Total Current Assets	5,839.77
Property/Plant/Equipment, Total - Gross	-
Accumulated Depreciation, Total	-
Goodwill, Net	5,406.47
Intangibles, Net	414.40
Long Term Investments	-
Other Long Term Assets, Total	139.89
Total Assets	12,697.25
Accounts Payable	88.02
Accrued Expenses	691.27
Notes Payable/Short Term Debt	0.00
Current Port. of LT Debt/Capital Leases	-
Other Current liabilities, Total	2,032.34
Total Current Liabilities	2,811.64
Long Term Debt	1,892.20
Capital Lease Obligations	-
Total Long Term Debt	1,892.20
Total Debt	1,892.20
Deferred Income Tax	217.66
Minority Interest	-
Other Liabilities, Total	350.92
Total Liabilities	5,272.41

fig. 31

Google and the Google logo are registered trademarks of Google Inc., used with permission.

The sum of WidgetCorp's total assets is 12.7 billion. Its total liability (debt) is 5.27 billion. In case you are wondering, a "current liability" simply means that the debt is due within a year, whereas other forms of liability are not due until after a year's time. By dividing our total liabilities (5.27B) by our total assets (12.7B) we come up with a debt ratio (debt-to-asset ratio) of .415. As a general rule, if a company's debt-to-asset ratio is below .5, then the company is thought to be in a strong financial position. If need be, it could sell off its assets and cover its debt at least two times over. This equates to less risk for investors. A more stable debt-to-asset ratio is to be expected from a company that has been around for a while and is pursuing a strategy of steady growth. Be careful, however, not to immediately dismiss a company just because it has a higher debt-to-asset ratio. A company that is younger or pursuing rapid expansion may need to take on new debt, and this is not necessarily a bad thing. It may even result in that company's stock soaring in the next few years. If a company you are interested in is loading up on debt, then you need to determine whether the company is capable of managing the debt in a sustainable fashion. Has the company managed similar levels of debt in the past? How fast were they able to reduce their debt ratio?

If a company has a solid track record when it comes to managing debt, then debt can be a good sign. The company may be marshaling together capital for a new and potentially profitable business endeavor. Buy! Buy! Buy! At your own risk, of course.

The debt-to-equity ratio is used by investors to assess the claims of creditors on a company's assets relative to the claims of shareholders.

Company ABC has issued a ton of corporate bonds. Meanwhile, the company's also issued stocks (and you are thinking about buying some shares). The company's debt-to-equity ratio should be assessed as a measure of risk. Before you buy, keep in mind that the corporate bondholders (along with banks and other creditors) will have first priority in the event the company needs to liquidate its assets.

Shareholders are essentially the business owners. If the debt-to-equity ratio is 3, then the company's creditors (bondholders and others) have a claim on its assets three times as strong as its equity holders (stockholders). The company's debt-to-equity ratio is usually featured prominently in summary data about its stock, but we can also use the company's balance sheet to make the calculation ourselves.

fig. 32

In Millions of USD (except for per share items)	
Redeemable Preferred Stock, Total	-
Preferred Stock - Non Redeemable, Net	0.00
Common Stock, Total	0.06
Additional Paid-In Capital	4,616.33
Retained Earnings (Accumulated Deficit)	8,114.52
Treasury Stock - Common	-5,132.47
Other Equity, Total	-173.60
Total Equity	7,424.84
Total Liabilities & Shareholders' Equity	12,697.25
Shares Outs - Common Stock Primary Issue	-
Total Common Shares Outstanding	494.25

Google and the Google logo are registered trademarks of Google Inc., used with permission.

Figure 32 is the equity section of the balance sheet. The total value of the company's equity is 7.42B. Now we need to take our total measurement of debt. From Figure 31 we know our total liability (short-term plus long-term debt) is 5.27B. Using these measurements, we find that our debt-to-equity ratio is .71. The company's creditors therefore have a 71 percent claim on every dollar in equity value held by the stockholders.

The concept of capital structure comes into play here. *Capital structure* refers to the mechanisms, relationships, and contracts a company establishes in order to secure capital. Figure 33 depicts a standard capital structure hierarchy.

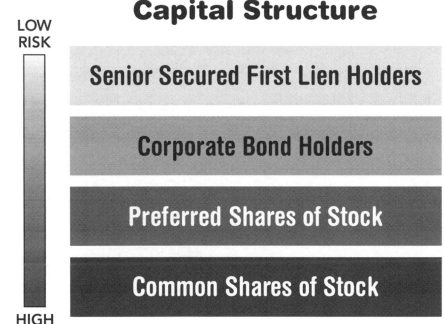

Capital Structure

LOW RISK

Senior Secured First Lien Holders

Corporate Bond Holders

Preferred Shares of Stock

Common Shares of Stock

HIGH RISK

GRAPHIC

fig. 33

Common shares of stock are at the very lowest point of the capital structure, meaning that common stock confers the most risk. If the company goes out of business, common stockholders will be least likely (relative to other capital suppliers) to have their money returned. Holders of preferred stock (see chapter 1) will be paid out before common stock shareholders, but they still hold significant risk because preferred stockholders are still in an equity position—they own a piece of the company. Bondholders do not, by virtue of their bonds, own the company. They have lent the company money, which the company has agreed to pay back with interest.

In the event of bankruptcy, liquidation, etc., the bondholders will be paid before any equity shareholders (owners of common and preferred stock). Bondholders are lenders; they don't "own it" if things go bad, at least not like equity shareholders do.

"Senior secured first lien holders" are in a less risky position relative to any of the other aforementioned capital suppliers. The capital lent to the company by these lien holders has been collateralized by the company's assets. In the event the company fails, the first lien holders will be able to repossess and liquidate company assets. In the event of a bankruptcy, the first lien holder's collateralized position is preferable to that of a bondholder whose bonds, if paid out at all, could be paid out at pennies on the dollar.

A senior secured first lien holder in a REIT may have a claim on the REIT's real estate holdings in the event the REIT becomes financially insolvent.

Some investors look for companies that have more debt because—assuming that they faithfully pay their bills, invest in profitable expansions, and steadily deleverage themselves—they will provide higher returns over time. More conservative investors and those that want big dividend payments will prefer companies with little or no debt. The former play, investing in companies with higher debt and hoping for a larger than average return, is considered an example of **growth investing**. Growth investors want to invest in companies that are making big moves in exciting and lucrative spaces. Growth investors are comfortable with more risk if it means more reward, and companies with higher debt-to-asset and debt-to-equity ratios are generally considered to be higher risk. The counterpart to growth investing is **value investing**. Value investors are looking for a good deal on a solid company. They conduct careful fundamental analyses and look for stocks that are selling below their market value. When a bad earnings report comes out about a stock and temporarily (so we think) depresses the price, the value investors will swoop in. They evaluate the company's financial fundamentals, and if they determine the current earnings report to be only a blip on the radar, they will buy in. Value investors want company earnings to go back to the investors. They are hot for stocks that pay higher dividends, and they are not so hot on companies that are using significant chunks of revenue to service debt.

The same Fama/French multiyear study that I have called upon several times throughout this text also conducted an analysis that pitted the returns of growth stocks against those of value stocks over time. We featured this graphic back in chapter 3, but here it is again in case you missed it.

Value Stocks vs. Growth Stocks According to Fama/French

GRAPHIC

fig. 34

Evaluation Period	Value Stocks Outperform Growth Stocks
1 year	61% of the time
5 year	77% of the time
10 year	88% of the time
15 year	97% of the time

In addition to the metrics discussed in this chapter and in this book as a whole, there is a vast universe of ratios and points of evaluation that can be used to inform investment decisions. We could literally fill an encyclopedia with the many ways in which these evaluation tools are used, and if you decide to pursue investing, you will undoubtedly learn more and more as you go. For now, let's take a quick look at a few other important metrics that you are sure to come across early in your investing career.

» **Price-to-Book Ratio (P/B)** – The P/B is the price of a company's stock shares divided by its tangible net assets. It is called price to book because the value of tangible assets, such as equipment, investments, and real estate, are recorded in a company's accounting books. Lower P/B ratios are favored among value investors, whereas growth investors will tolerate a higher P/B.

» **Price/Earnings to Growth (PEG)** – The PEG ratio divides the P/E ratio by the growth of earnings per share over a given time period. The purpose of this ratio is to give investors a way to consider growth trends alongside earnings trends. The lower the PEG ratio, the more valuable the stock.

» **Free Cash Flow (FCF)** – Free cash flow is the amount of cash a company has on hand after paying off all capital and general expenses. This leftover cash is used to pay dividends to shareholders, pay down debt, buy back stock, and expand business activity. A company with high FCF may have greater flexibility, but a company with a lower or even negative FCF is not necessarily failing. It may just be making major investments.

To build your proficiencies using these and other investment metrics, begin by choosing a market sector in which you have a particular interest. Learn how capital, debt, cash, and other factors work in that particular sector. Study the different companies that compete in the sector and their financial metrics relative to one another. Meanwhile, stay abreast of industry and economic news that can have an effect on stock prices.

ON THE MOST USEFUL STOCK EVALUATION METRICS: I like to search out value stocks with P/E ratios lower than those of comparable stocks. If I can identify a stock that is priced too low relative to its peers, then the next thing I look at is the dividend yield percentage. The percentage will often be higher on undervalued stocks, as a greater proportion of the company's cash is being returned to the stock's investors. To me, this signals a value stock worth considering as a buying opportunity.

The Importance of Patience in Long-Term Investing

Taking a loss is one of the most important things you can experience as a newcomer to investing. You buy a stock and it rewards you by steadily declining in value. This is an important experience, because you may take a lot of losses on your road to being successful. Spectacular success in investing is not possible if you are too afraid to make mistakes. Even Warren Buffett takes losses. It comes with the territory.

We have already discussed how the constant monitoring of your portfolio can be detrimental to your well-being. The movement of a day, a week, or even a few months is hardly consequential in the world of long-term investing. Trust in your investments and give them the time they need to work for you. If you are reactive and trade away your positions at the first sign of trouble, then you will end up paying too much in trading commissions while sacrificing the possibility of long-term gains. Worse still, you will soon find a new way to make yourself crazy by tracking the investments you prematurely sold and agonizing over those that end up soaring high in the long term.

Regardless of the stage of your development as an investor, you will be called upon to exert patience, discipline, and acceptance. From taking your first loss to sitting on your cash as you wait for a deal that is worth taking action on, don't expect to be a perfect investor. Perfection is impossible, but competence is very much within reach.

If you are going to trade stocks, especially if you intend to trade individual companies, then it is important to set rules for yourself to instruct your behavior during downside movements. Preservation of capital is important, so stick to a defined maximum loss percentage and ensure you do not exceed it. For example, 10 percent might be an appropriate maximum loss percentage for some investors; if you invest $1,000 in a stock and the value of the stock declines to $900 (-10%), then you would cut your losses and exit the position.

You can also use maximum loss percentage tactics to secure your profits. If your $1,000 investment climbs to $1,500 in value, you can reset your 10 percent maximum loss percentage; if the investment then drops to $1,350 (-10%), you would sell and keep the $350 in profit.

Stop-loss orders (chapter 1) can be used to automatically exit positions when their value declines by an amount you specify.

A 10 percent maximum loss percentage is but one example of a rule that you can set for yourself to help you stay disciplined during your investment journey. Whatever rules you set for yourself should, of course, be adhered to, and should integrate sensibly with your overall investment plan and objectives. Remember to invest with discipline and to avoid forming emotional attachments to your investments. Rather than committing yourself to any one particular investment position, commit instead to the ongoing financial well-being of yourself and your loved ones.

Chapter Recap

» There are a variety of metrics and tools available to help investors identify stocks they would like to buy.

» Factors such as interest rates, political stability, employment rates, and taxes can influence the prices of stocks.

» Investments in emerging and international markets should be considered when pursuing a healthy, risk-resilient, and diversified portfolio.

» Fundamental analysis evaluates the strength of the underlying asset, while technical analysis focuses on the immediate factors affecting price movement in a stock.

» Metrics such as debt-to-asset ratio (debt ratio) and debt-to-equity ratio help investors assess investment risk.

» Growth investors are willing to take on more risk in exchange for higher returns, while value investors prefer a company with strong fundamentals poised to offer steady, reliable returns.

| 5 |
Investment Strategies

I will tell you how to become rich. Close the doors. Be fearful when others are greedy. Be greedy when others are fearful.

— WARREN BUFFETT

Though investment strategies are formed and function within the shared norms of the financial world, they are no less personal and original investor by investor. Your own investment strategy should be based on many factors, including your tolerance for risk, your investment goals, the industries with which you are most familiar, the amount of time you intend to spend researching investment opportunities, and the amounts and frequencies with which you expect your investments to produce yields.

In this chapter we are going to go over a few basic investment strategies that are both simple and powerful. These strategies can help you form a strong strategic foundation as you pursue the development of your own unique investing style.

Buying on Down Days

Contrarianism is an investment approach whereby the investor attempts to gauge the sentiment of the market at large and to behave in the opposite way. If everyone else is buying bonds, then you buy stocks. If transportation sector stocks are hitting record highs, then you diminish their presence in your portfolio by selling some off. If the price of a blue chip stock takes a steep hit following a bad earnings report, then it is a great time to think about buying a few shares.

It was my own belief in the value of investment contrarianism that led me to load up on international stocks back in 2014, both for myself and for my clients. Since the US economy was doing so well, money was flowing out of international investments. The financial media was downplaying the value of international stocks.[47] All the naysaying drove down prices. It was the perfect time to buy.

You do not have to be an exceptional student of financial history to see that international stocks, like most other major stock categories, go up and down, sometimes staying down, or up, for years at a time before moving in the opposite direction. While patient, disciplined investors will anticipate these imminent tidal shifts, many investors are neither patient nor disciplined. In the same way that some people cannot stand the sight of their own blood, many investors cannot stand to hold on to investments that have been stagnant or losing money for several years. It is an understandable, though irrational, sentiment. It is easier for investors like me, who have been exposed intimately to the ebbs and flows of the market for decades at a time, to build a more vivid awareness of persistent, long-term, broad-based market realities. What goes down usually goes back up.

One of the simplest and most effective investment strategies is to make big purchases of stock on down days and during down periods. The underlying assumption here is that most stocks recover, and the markets always recover. That is not just wishful thinking but historical fact. Now, if you are anxious to get your money in the market and you have cash sitting around doing nothing, especially if interest rates are low, then it may be difficult for you to be patient enough to wait for a down market. Keep in mind, though, that the cash you have parked in a savings account (let's say it is earning 1 percent in annual interest [low interest rate environment]), has value in the form of opportunity. By holding onto your cash, you have the chance to act when a great opportunity presents itself. For older investors especially, who are already inclined to keep more of their investments in cash or cash equivalents, finding cash to spend in a down market should not be too difficult. If need be, you can liquidate a few bonds. If the economy has taken a downward turn and you have bonds that were bought in a healthy economy, their value will likely be higher than the bonds being issued in the down economy. You can sell these healthy, higher-yield bonds at a profit and invest the cash in the stock market.

If you are still feeling a little shaky about making stock market purchases in a down economy, then you can buy stocks in sectors most resistant to recession, such as healthcare and consumer staples. The prices for these stocks will likely have been driven down along with the rest of the market, but because they generate healthy cash flows, even during recessions, they are not as likely to go bankrupt or to become overly dependent on opportunistic, high-interest creditors. Other industries that keep the cash flowing during recessions include weapons manufacturers, alcohol-related companies, and tobacco stocks.

If you would prefer to stay clear of "sin stocks," then you may find stable investments in other spaces such as telecom, utilities, and consumer staples, to name a few. A more in-depth review of ethical considerations when investing can be found in chapter 8. Preferred stocks (see chapter 1) are also thought to offer stability and some dependability during times of economic stagnation or recession.

Dollar Cost Averaging

Dollar cost averaging (DCA) is a smart way to ease your way into an investment at a potentially optimal cost.

Let's say that we have completed a fundamental analysis on Boingo Wireless Inc (WIFI). We conclude that even though the stock's had a rough time the previous year, it is a solid long-term investment, and its recent struggles will probably ensure that we get a good price.

We decide we are going to invest about $1,000 in WIFI stock, but we are not in a huge hurry to load up all at once. Using the dollar cost averaging strategy, we can gradually invest in the stock and ensure that we get the lowest possible price. Here's how it works. We select a buying period, let's say one year. During the course of this year, we are going to invest about $1,000 in WIFI, but rather than do it all at once via one purchase, we are going to split up the purchase into twelve monthly installments of about $83.33 ($1,000/12).

If WIFI is trading at $16 during our first month, then we will buy five shares, a total spend of $80. The next month—let's say WIFI is trading at $13—we will buy six shares. The following month it might be trading at $14 and we will buy six shares again. We keep doing this for twelve months until we spend our $1,000 allotment.

In theory, dollar cost averaging allows investors to purchase more shares in a stock for the same amount of money.

Over the course of twelve months, we have spent $1,000 and purchased 67 shares of WIFI. If we spent that same $1,000 in the first month when the stock was priced at $16, we would only have been able to purchase 62 shares. Since the price of the stock ended up back at $17, five extra shares represents $85 more in value.

Dollar Cost Average Strategy for WIFI Purchase

fig. 35

MONTH	JAN	FEB	MAR	APR	MAY	JUN
Money Spent	≈ $83.33	≈ $83.33	≈ $83.33	≈ $83.33	≈ $83.33	≈ $83.33
Stock Price	$16	$13	$14	$12	$14	$18
Shares Purchased	5	6	6	7	6	5

MONTH	JUL	AUG	SEP	OCT	NOV	DEC
Money Spent	≈ $83.33	≈ $83.33	≈ $83.33	≈ $83.33	≈ $83.33	≈ $83.33
Stock Price	$20	$16	$12	$13	$17	$17
Shares Purchased	4	5	7	6	5	5

Dollar cost averaging does not, by any means, guarantee investors more bang for their buck. If you have the cash to invest and you choose to gradually enter into a position over time, there is always the risk that you will end up paying more for fewer shares than you would have paid had you invested all at once. Furthermore, anytime you pursue a strategy where you are making more frequent trades, you will incur added expense in the form of commissions and fees. In our WIFI example above, the investor would have to factor in the costs of the twelve trades, one each month over the course of a year. If each trade costs $5 ($60 in total), then the $250 value of the strategy must be reduced to $190.

Q: Is the dollar cost averaging strategy more likely to be successful in an up market or a down market? What do you think?

Consider the following scenario: you have a thousand dollars to invest every month, and you decide to use the dollar cost averaging (DCA) strategy to gradually buy into a stock that is currently selling for $10 per share. Figure 36 depicts how this strategy could play out in two different market environments.

In the first environment (the "rising cycle") the stock is steadily climbing in value. In the second environment (the "fluctuating cycle") the stock declines and then gradually regains strength.

Which Market is Best for DCA

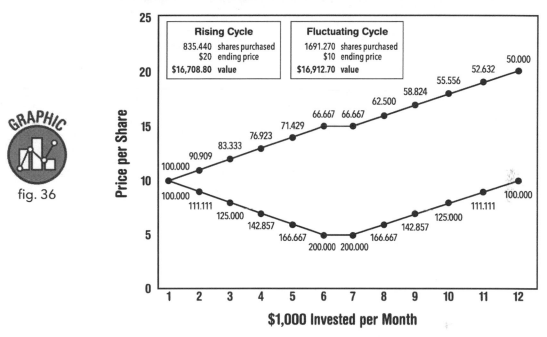

At the end of twelve months, the use of DCA in the fluctuating cycle resulted in the more valuable position, $16,912.70 versus $16,708.80. This is because the investor in the fluctuating cycle was able to purchase more shares at a faster pace. By the end of the twelve-month period, the fluctuating cycle investor bought about twice as many shares as the rising cycle investor. Because the fluctuating cycle investor was able to acquire more shares throughout the period, he was positioned to reap greater net benefits when the stock began to climb in price, enough to surpass the rising cycle investor despite the fact that the stock itself was worth twice as much at the end of the rising cycle. At the end of the day it is share count, not stock price, that is the essential catalyst for generating wealth. You can quote me on that.

Dollar cost averaging is a good tool for investors who are new to investing or particularly cautious about a certain investment and want to test the waters before they plunge right in. If a stock is particularly volatile, dollar cost averaging can be used to help ensure that you do not put in all your money at the peak of the stock's price. Using a DCA strategy can also serve to insulate you from a major market crash or correction. Investing a huge lump sum of cash into the market right before it goes down is incredibly demoralizing. Keep in mind that even though the market steadily rises with time, the downturns can be sudden and steep. A good way to assess whether DCA is a good strategy for a particular investment is by taking into account the amount you want to invest relative to the total amount of investable cash you have on hand. If you have a significant quantity of cash and plan on moving a lot of it into the market, then you may want to do it gradually via DCA. If you are looking to invest only 5 percent of the investable cash you have on hand, then a lump sum investment may be the best way to proceed.

Assuming you are investing directly out of your cash supply (as opposed to trading out of other equity positions), the DCA approach may help limit your risk exposure in the event of a sudden crash and may possibly help you purchase more shares for less money during the downturn. Contrarily, DCA may result in lost dividend payments (if you are not fully invested, then you will not receive dividends) and you also risk losing out on potential capital gains if the market goes up while you are executing your DCA strategy.

A helpful variation on the DCA approach is to adjust your investment installments based on the value of the stock. This is known as "value averaging." Let's say you are resolved to invest $10,000 in stock over the course of a year. You invest $833 (1/12 of $10,000) the first month. The next month, the stock drops by 15 percent, so your $833 investment is now worth $708. Your investment is worth less, but the stock is less expensive. Using the value averaging approach, you are going to invest your $833 *plus* $125 for your next installment of $958. The $125 figure is derived by subtracting the current value of the investment, $708, from your initial investment amount, $833. If your investment increases rather than decreases in value, then you do the opposite. Let's say our investment increased in value by 15 percent in month two, from $833 to $958. Rather than invest an extra $125 during month two, we will invest $125 *less*, since the stock is now more expensive. In theory, if we continue to pursue this strategy over the course of a year, we will end up paying less money to own more shares of a stock we believe will be a long-term winner.

Value averaging, like DCA, is a long-term strategy and requires guts and confidence in the longer-term strength of the stock. Again, these approaches may not be necessary if you are not investing a significant amount of money. If you do pursue these strategies, prepare to stay disciplined and stick to your plan. It is not easy to keep putting more and more money into an investment after you have watched it decline in value for three months running. However, throughout your experience as an investor, you will often discover that what is right is often counterintuitive. We will talk more about separating emotion from sound strategy in chapter 7.

Analyze, Group, & Qualify

Perhaps the easiest, safest, and most reliable way to realize good returns from the stock market is to pick solid positions and stick with them for the long term. The question then becomes, "How do I pick the right stocks?" And the answer is not exactly easy, but—good news!—it is also not terribly difficult. When building the core of your portfolio, focus on industries that will inevitably endure and be in higher demand over time. Healthcare stocks come to mind. Considering that we have an aging population, the healthcare sector will likely be forced to expand. Expansion, when managed competently, will possibly yield higher market capitalization, more earnings, and higher stock prices. If you believe that the healthcare industry will endure and expand with time, then you can either invest in a pre-diversified healthcare-focused ETF or mutual fund, or you can choose a few stocks from the sectors you think are the most likely to prosper. Do this by conducting a fundamental analysis of the stock (see chapter 4). Learn all you can about the company's current leadership, the projects it is pursuing, and its financial well-being. Look for healthy levels of debt and a good track record of growth. Invest in a handful of companies, if possible.

If you are interested in being more of a hands-on investor, then you should diligently follow the industries and companies in which you are invested.

Stock prices will go up and down. Your time is best spent studying financial reports and news about the companies and industries in which you are invested or in which you plan to invest.

Becoming an expert in a few sectors will allow you to intelligently improve and expand on your positions and make good trades, and it may even open the door for you to leverage options and other shorter-term instruments within your target industry (see chapter 6).

Another fun and often effective way of picking out stocks for the long term is identifying new technologies or trends you believe will persevere and grow, and investigating the companies that are engaging in these trends.

Let's say you are a die-hard gamer (video games) and believe wholeheartedly in the promise of virtual reality (VR) as the future of gaming. If you believe in the VR trend, then your first step toward making an investment is identifying the major players in the space. You will soon learn that Facebook purchased the much-hyped Oculus VR company in March of 2014. They paid about two billion dollars in stock and cash for the company[48] in a deal that left many investors scratching their heads.

Oculus VR is not yet at a point where it is generating a great deal of revenue. The play by Facebook was essentially the same as a play by any investor (like you, perhaps), who believes VR will expand over time. Judging by Facebook's stock performance immediately following the Oculus VR acquisition, the market appears to have responded unfavorably out of the gate. In the three weeks following the acquisition, the value of FB declined, close to 20 percent (an ideal time to make an investment!).

fig. 37

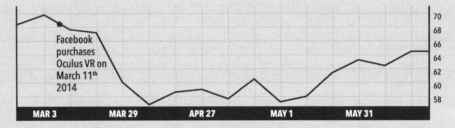

Google and the Google logo are registered trademarks of Google Inc., used with permission. Stock Value for Facebook Inc. – March 2014 through June 2014

From 2014 to 2017, however, the stock's value doubled.

fig. 38

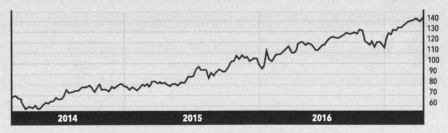

Google and the Google logo are registered trademarks of Google Inc., used with permission. Stock Value for Facebook Inc. – March 2014 through April 2017

Now, the initial 20 percent fall-off (Figure 37) is probably far more relevant to the Oculus VR purchase than the subsequent doubling of FB over several years' time (Figure 38). Remember, Oculus VR was purchased for a paltry two-billion-dollar sum, which is less than 1 percent of Facebook's 416-billion-dollar market cap value (as of April 2017). There is very little likelihood that such a small acquisition would contribute significantly to a sustained three-year growth trend.

If investors reacted to the purchase at all, they reacted to a news headline ('FB purchases Oculus'), not to any substantial and enduring change in the company's core fundamentals. And the fact that they immediately reacted poorly to a technology that we believe has huge, game-changing (pun intended) potential would have been good news for us, if we had been fortunate enough to purchase shares in FB immediately following the announcement.

After all, the value of Oculus could grow significantly over the longer term. Cantor Fitzgerald, a New York City-based financial services firm that counts gaming tech among their specialties, agrees with this assessment of virtual reality, predicting a thirty-billion-dollar market by 2020. By that time, they predict, Facebook will be deriving 10 percent of its revenue from Oculus VR sales.[49] Having Cantor Fitzgerald in your corner as you assess the market can't hurt. Ten percent of all revenue generation in a 400+ billion dollar company is serious business. Maybe we should go ahead and jump on the VR train now (via FB) despite the high share price. Then again, maybe we should proceed with caution.

Before we go and blow our entire virtual/augmented reality investment budget on Facebook, we have to look at the possible downsides. For starters, there is a lawsuit in progress being waged against Facebook by video game giant ZeniMax, alleging that certain key developments that led to the creation of Oculus's VR technology were undertaken by a former ZeniMax employee, and that this work was improperly shared with Oculus's founders. It's bad. They have evidence of a steady stream of proprietary code being transmitted from ZeniMax to Oculus for several months. ZeniMax is even going so far as to show that their former employee was Googling information on how to thoroughly wipe a hard drive immediately after he received notice of ZeniMax's intent to pursue litigation.[50]

Even though it is an ugly lawsuit and has the potential to create some serious drag on the sales timeline (the Cantor Fitzgerald analysis predates the legal drama by about nine months), the result will likely be no more than an expensive settlement for Oculus VR / Facebook. Conclusion: this lawsuit is not going to sink our whole play, but we should definitely check out some competitors in the VR space before we make any big purchases. Google has been steadily rolling out its augmented reality (Google Glass) and virtual reality (Google Cardboard) technologies. Stock in Google's holding company, Alphabet Inc. (GOOG), continues to climb with each passing year. Microsoft (MSFT) is another steady all-around performer poised to make a splash in VR. Microsoft's HoloLens was introduced at the 2015 Game Developers' Conference.[51] We might be safer following the conventional wisdom of diversification, investing in a basket of securities that have VR development on their horizons.

Another factor to consider when deciding on which stock to buy, and how much, is the behavior of other investors. It is always nice to discover that professional investors are of like mind when it comes to your stock selections. One of the best ways to track the decisions of investment pros is through hedge funds, aka the most *actively managed* of all actively managed funds. Hedge fund traders are constantly under pressure to find ways to improve the performance of their funds, so they have a very high level of activity. Sites like HedgeMind.com[52] allow investors to monitor the behavior of various hedge fund management firms.

Figure 39[53] is a heat map showing recent hedge fund stock activity surrounding Alphabet Inc. (GOOG). As you can see, not all hedge fund managers are going to see the market the same way. Dinakar Singh's firm just sold all of its Google stock, while George Soros just bought 12,700 new shares.

It is harder to find day-to-day info on longer-term investors like Warren Buffett, perhaps because they do not generate as much trading activity as the typical hedge fund. Nonetheless, when Buffett or some other investing legend makes a big purchase or sells

fig. 39

William Johnson ITHAKA GROUP LLC	
38,797 SH	-6,570 SH
4.74%	-14.45% sold

Dinakar Singh TPG-AXON MANAGEMENT LP	
29,881 SH	-29,881 SH
2.98%	-100% sold

Sol Kurnin FOLGER HILL ASSET MANAGEMENT LP	
25,158 SH	-20 SH
1.17%	-0.08% sold

John Burbank III PASSPORT CAPITAL LLC	
18,723 SH	+10,384 SH
0.3%	55.46% new

George Soros SOROS FUND MANAGEMENT LLC	
12,700 SH	+12,700 SH
0.25%	100% new

something off, you will usually read about it on the front page of the business news.

ON FOLLOWING THE PLAYS OF BIG-TIME INVESTORS: In the finance industry it is often quite difficult to pick out the next big star. If you were able to somehow identify the next great investor and copy her plays before she became famous, then yeah, you would stand to profit significantly. The trouble with simply copying the plays of already-well-known investors is that you are going to be coming in on the back end of their success. For one thing, they already have a fan base that instantly bids up the prices of their picks after they are made public. These artificial price swings will cut into your profit margins, even if the famous investor continues to achieve long-term success, which is not guaranteed.

Bear Market Strategies

We have said time and again—and you will hear this advice echoed throughout the financial advisement landscape—do not try to time the market. That said, there are strategies you can use to reasonably limit losses. If you think a major market downturn is imminent, simply put stop-loss orders on your stocks, so that they will automatically sell in the event of a downturn. During normal times, placing a stop-loss of about 10-15 percent may be appropriate, depending on how volatile the stock is and how far down you are willing to go. So if your stock is selling for $100, then you would place a stop-loss order with a stop price of $90 (10%) or $85 (15%). If you think the market is due for a major collapse, then a 5 percent stop-loss may be more appropriate.

You may not want to set a stop-loss order too close to the current price, because you may trigger the sell order faster than you intended, only to see the stock value quickly recover. Instead, you should strategically position your stop-loss orders at stop prices that protect you from substantial loss, but not so close to the current price that you risk being whipsawed in and out of the market.

Some investors prefer not to use a formal stop-loss order, but rather to monitor their stocks directly and then issue a standard sell order when the stock falls below their stop price.

Even if you have a stop-loss order for a stock, your broker will not make any guarantee that they will be able to sell the stock for the price you have specified. They make their commissions simply for brokering the trade; therefore, there is no incentive for them to go the extra mile to ensure that you get the best possible price. If you prefer not to use stop-loss orders, you can use personal text messaging or email alerts instead. Most brokers will allow you to request notification in the event a stock drops (or climbs) to a price you specify. After you are alerted, you can initiate a standard limit order to sell your stock(s), which will force your broker to make the transaction at the price you have specified. If they cannot find a buyer, then they will not get a commission.

Your exit strategy depends on a lot of factors, including the volatility of the stock and the purpose of the investment. When you conduct your fundamental and technical analysis of a stock prior to your initial purchase, you should also begin considering an exit strategy to limit losses in the event the stock goes sour. If you bail out too soon, then you risk selling your position prematurely, but if you sell too late, you will take more than you need to in losses.

For investors willing to stake their lot on the doom and gloom that is *surely* lurking just around the corner, there are things called "bear market funds." These funds use short selling and other strategies that have the potential to produce big returns in down markets. Bear market funds are often misused by investors who see them as a place to turn to in the midst of a downturn, when all of their other positions are quickly losing value. Desperate to make some return on the downward trend, they end up throwing a bunch of money into a bear fund in the hope that the worst is yet to come. The more mature bear fund investor uses the fund as a hedge against a market downturn. During a normal market, the fund is going to lose 10 percent or so of its value annually, but will provide a nice cushion in a down market. In this way bear market funds are meant to operate as a kind of portfolio insurance. You pay a little bit every year in exchange for a lifeline during tough times. If you are not familiar with short selling as an investment tactic, a more thorough review of the topic is available in the following chapter.

Chapter Recap

» Keeping a cash reserve, even in the midst of a bull market, gives investors a chance to buy stocks at a discount in the event of a sudden downturn.

» Dollar cost averaging allows investors to gradually enter into a position; it may in some scenarios result in the acquisition of more shares for the same amount of money.

» Studying various industries, identifying macro-level trends, and checking your investment decisions against those of highly reputed investment professionals can all help to inform a sound strategy.

» Bear market funds, when properly utilized, act as insurance bets to insulate your portfolio in the event of a severe market downturn.

| 6 |
The Short Game
Speculating, Risk-Taking, & Embracing the Drama

Chapter Overview
» Options Trading
» Penny Stocks
» Futures
» Other Higher Risk Investments

Derivatives are financial weapons of mass destruction.

– WARREN BUFFETT

Investors and traders are the two major actors in the stock market. The typical investor buys and holds, in hopes of realizing substantial gains over time. A trader, by contrast, buys and sells, or even sells and then buys in the case of a short sell. Also, traders are often more inclined to buy or sell security **derivatives**, such as options or futures contracts, that obligate the purchase or sale of a certain quantity of a certain security at a certain date. A trader is much more concerned with the day-by-day and hour-by-hour investor sentiment toward a security. He is less concerned with the nature of the underlying asset or any financial fundamentals. Traders make money by staking out a position, profiting, and liquidating, all at breakneck speeds. For a trader, stock market volatility is a good thing. There is tremendous profit to be gained (and fast) by predicting the dramatic movement of a stock price. If only it were easy to do. It's not.

The truth about trading is that it is a lot easier to lose money than it is to make money. Multiple sources have documented that less than 10 percent of traders end up being profitable. Many analysts say that 10 percent is too optimistic and the real number is closer to 1 percent. Trading requires a much greater frequency of transactions than investing. More trades mean more commissions and fees paid to brokers and more **slippage costs**. Slippage refers to the tick or two of lost value that frequently occurs when exiting a position.

You may have a plan to get out as soon as the stock hits $65, but because of slippage, your actual exit price may end up being a bit lower. The expense of frequent trading adds up quickly. Traders who want to profit have to possess the ability to consistently interpret the data properly and make sure their money is on the right side of the fence. This requires a level of proficiency, particularly in technical analysis, that can take many years to achieve.

Trading occasionally as a hobby with very limited knowledge about what you are doing is essentially speculating. You may post some big wins, but if you think you have found your new career calling, proceed with caution and humility. Researchers at the University of California, Berkeley, found that traders tend to over-attribute their trading successes to their innate abilities, leading to overconfidence and longer-term financial losses.[54] Trading can be exciting and fun, and there is nothing wrong with that. But it is wise to maintain clear expectations about the long-term financial results you are likely to achieve.

In this chapter we will review some of the most popular modes of trading, many of which, such as options trading, can be incorporated by certain investors into more traditional investment strategies.

Day Trading

Day trading refers to the buying and selling of securities within a same-day period. This approach to stock market investing stands in stark contrast to the traditional "buy-and-hold" approach used by long-term investors. The "dedicated day trader" is a term that has emerged to describe an investment professional or entrepreneur who works as a full-time trader. Though many would-be professional day traders are allured by the fast-paced lifestyle—who wouldn't be interested in seizing thousands of dollars in profit during the course of a few hours—very few who enter the field end up profiting from it. Most lose significant sums of money relative to their initial investments.

If you are involved in stock trading in any depth, then you will likely be subject to the siren call of brokerages promoting day trading and promising quick and easy fortunes. These sales pitches are quite prevalent in the financial media. It is important to consider the incentives of brokerages that promote day trading. Brokerages make their money by taking commissions off of stock purchasing or selling transactions. The more you trade, the more they make. Day traders, therefore, are prime clientele.

Day traders look for stocks that have high levels of price volatility and liquidity. If the trader can predict the direction of a significant price swing (volatility), then the opportunity for profit is greater. Liquidity is important to ensure that the stocks can be readily bought and sold. What good is seeing the value of a stock surge or sink in the direction you predicted when you are unable to get your trade through?

Several of the trading markets discussed in this chapter are go-to haunts for day traders, such as the options, Forex, and futures markets. Short selling and buying on margin (also discussed in this chapter) are day trading staples.[d]

Options Trading

Options trading is based on the buying and selling of options contracts. An options contract gives an investor the right to buy or sell a security, at a specified price, within a specified window of time. As time passes, the value of the options contract is subject to change. The value of the options contract also fluctuates, often quite dramatically, in response to the changes in value of the underlying security.

You purchase an options contract that will allow you to buy a specific dress for a price of $100 at any time within the next nine months. You pay $50 to own this options contract. This is known as the "premium." Let's say that the dress was selling for $125 at the time you bought the contract. If you wanted to exercise your option right away, you could, but you would not profit. You would have spent a total of $150 to own the dress ($100 to buy the dress per the dictates of the contract plus a $50 premium to procure the options contract). It would have been better for you to simply buy the dress outright for $125.

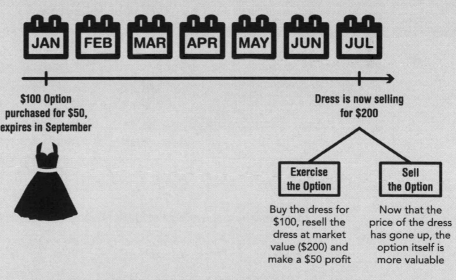

fig. 40

But let's say that six months after you purchase the options contract, the dress is modeled by Kate Middleton in a high-end fashion catalog. The dress is now selling for $200 and you still own the options contract. If you exercise your options contract, then you will profit $50. That is, you buy the dress for $100, the price specified in your options contract, and immediately resell it at its new market value of $200, a difference of $100. Then you subtract the $50 premium you paid to own the option, and you are left with a $50 profit.

In another scenario, Kate Middleton models the dress, the price goes up to $200, and rather than buying the dress, you simply sell the options contract to another party. Remember, when you bought the $100 option for $50, the dress was selling for $125. Now that the dress is selling for $200, your $100 option, which does not expire for another three months, is going to be worth a lot more than the $50 you paid for it six months ago.

Replace the dress in our example with stocks and other securities, and you have options trading in a nutshell. Options trading markets can be complicated and fast-paced environments that are not conducive to the interests of many beginner-level or conservative-minded investors. Day traders are often avid options traders as well, because volatility and liquidity play major roles in options trading just as they do in standard day trading.

The standard options trading vernacular centers around calls and puts. A **call option** is written/sold by the owner of a security. The buyer (owner) of a call option buys the right to purchase the stock at a specific price within a specific window of time. A **put option** is written (sold) by a trader willing to promise the purchase of a particular security at a specific price within a specific window of time. The buyer (owner) of a put option has the right to sell shares of the security at the price specified any time within the specified window.

If you are confused, think of it this way—if you buy (own) a call option (like we did in the dress example), then you are buying the right to *call* in a stock (security) at an agreed-upon price (like we did when we called in the dress for $100 in July despite the fact that its July market price was $200). We owned the call option and we used it. Reflexively, if you buy (own) a put option, then you have the right to *put* the stock back into the market at a specific price.

Here are the essentials of options strategy:

» When you *buy* a call option, you want the stock's price to go up.
» When you *sell* a call option, you want the stock's price to stay the same or go down.
» When you *buy* a put option, you want the stock's price to go down.
» When you *sell* a put option, you want the stock's price to stay the same or go up.

Let's say you buy a $100 put option rather than a $100 call option on the dress from the previous example. This put option would prove practically worthless if the price shot up to $200. You would still have the right to sell the dress for $100, but why would you want to? In order to do so you would first have to buy the dress at its current market price ($200). You would be out $100 plus the premium you paid to own the option. Not good. On the flip side, if something happened causing the price of the dress to go down to $50, then your put option (let's say you paid a $25 premium to own it) would be profitable! You would be able to buy the dress at its current market price ($50) then exercise the $100 put option to sell the dress for $100. After deducting the premium you paid to buy the option ($25) you would be left with a $25 profit.

The main factors affecting the premium you pay for any given option are, of course, the current value of the underlying security and the total duration of the contract. The longer the duration of the contract, the higher the premium.

Options are not used only by day traders. Traditional investors, especially higher-net-worth individuals who have significant sums of money in the markets, can leverage options trading. One common application is known as selling a *covered call*. A covered call option simply means that the writer (seller) already owns sufficient shares in the underlying security so as to cover all obligations in the event that the option is exercised by the buyer.

I have 100 shares of Company ABC stock (ABC), and I write a call option that guarantees another party the right to purchase 100 ABC shares for $54 per share at any time within the next three months. This is a covered call, because I already own the shares that I am committing to sell. Now, let's say that ABC is selling for $53 at the time that I write this option. The $54 "strike price" of my option is a dollar higher than the current value of the underlying asset ($53). In order for the buyer of my option to profit, ABC will have to go up in value. The buyer pays a premium of 50 cents per share. At 100 shares, that is $50 he is paying me to own the right to buy ABC from me at $54 a share at any time over the next three months.

Options contracts are typically for purchases of 100 shares (1 contract = 100 shares).

Selling a call option against shares that you already own, also known as selling a covered call, is one of the more conservative options strategies.

As an investor, why would I be attracted to the idea of writing a covered call option? Well, perhaps I am looking to sell off the underlying asset (the stock) and I am perfectly comfortable doing so at the strike price specified in the covered call option I am writing. Rather than simply sell out of a position, why not collect some premium income in the meantime by writing covered calls? If the stock does not go up and the option is not exercised, then I will happily hold onto the premium payment. If I want to, I can keep writing call options until one of them gets exercised and called away from me. The result is that I am out of the position, and I have collected some extra revenue in the meantime. The risk is that the stock spikes in value, beyond the strike price for the call option I wrote, and I would have made more money selling out of the position at its new market price than at the strike price for the call.

It is important to be aware of relevant tax implications when selling covered calls or engaging in any other type of options trading. Premiums received for selling covered calls are generally treated as short-term capital gains (see chapter 3). When call options are purchased and then exercised, resulting in the acquiring of a security, the cost basis (see chapter 1) for owning that security should include the premium paid to own the option. The 1099 form that your brokerage sends you at the end of the tax year may not incorporate the tax implications of your options trades. It is up to you to maintain your records and to properly account for any tax liabilities and tax benefits arising from your options trades. If you are new to options trading and unsure of how to manage the associated tax implications, then consult your tax advisor or CPA.

Ours is a very simplistic example of how options trading can be used to aid in more traditional investing practices. There are many complex options-based strategies that investors use to mitigate losses and expand gains. Many of these strategies involve writing or buying multiple options on the same stock. In fact, there are several basic strategies used by options traders that involve taking two different, and sometimes opposite, positions. The "straddle" strategy, for instance, requires that a put and a call option be purchased for the same stock at the same strike price. The "strangle" strategy also involves purchasing both a put and a call option on the same stock, though the put strike price will usually be lower than the call strike price. For a deeper dive into options trading[e], check out ClydeBank Finance's best-selling *Options Trading QuickStart Guide*.

Buying Stocks on Margin

Many brokers are willing to lend investors a portion of the cash they need to purchase stock. Making stock purchases in this way is known as "buying on margin." The investor will be responsible for paying back the borrowed amount to the brokerage along with commissions, fees, and interest. Investors choose to buy on margin because it is an opportunity for a greater return on investment.

Consider the following scenario: a stock is trading at $50 per share and you decide to purchase 100 shares. Rather than pay $5,000, you buy on margin and pay $2,500, borrowing the additional $2,500 from your broker. (According to the SEC's "Regulation T," no more than 50 percent of any margin purchase may be lent). If the stock goes up to $75, then your 100 shares are now worth $7,500. After paying back the principal you borrowed from your broker ($2,500), you will have $5,000 remaining—double the amount you originally paid to buy on margin ($2,500). You have netted a 100 percent return (minus interest and commission fees). Had you used only your own money to purchase the 100 shares of stock, then you would have only a 50 percent return on your investment.

Buying stocks on margin is a form of **leverage**, which refers to using borrowed money at a fixed interest rate to exert greater magnitudes of financial power. When you borrow money from the bank to purchase a home, you are leveraging the financial power of the bank to accomplish more than you could by relying only on your own supply of cash. Similarly, companies leverage their stockholders and bondholders in order to control larger amounts of capital. When you buy stocks on margin, you are leveraging your broker in order to purchase more stock for less money up front. If you are right about the stock, then your result will be a larger gain procured by a smaller upfront investment. If you are wrong, however, then you could be facing big losses, beyond just the loss of what you have already invested.

If we invest on margin and the stock falls in value, we are still on the hook for paying back the brokerage for what we borrowed, plus interest and commissions. After the stock drops below a certain point, the brokerage may issue what is called a "margin call." When a margin call is issued, the investor must either shore up his brokerage account with cash, or sell the stock, pay back the broker for all borrowed amounts, and write the rest off as a loss.

Interest on stocks purchased on margin accumulates with time, making margin purchases ill-suited for longer-term investments. In order to purchase stocks on margin you need to have at least $2,000 worth of cash or securities available to trade, depending on your brokerage firm. Your brokerage has the right to liquidate these assets if need be to cover loan repayments.[f,g]

Short Selling

Short selling is a practice used by investors who want to bet against the performance of a certain stock or other security. When the value of the security goes down, the investors who have "shorted" the stock will gain money. As with buying on margin, short selling involves borrowing shares from your brokerage and obliging yourself to pay back interest. Short selling is also, like buying on margin, risky business. If the stock you short goes up in value, then your losses could be, theoretically, limitless.

When an investor shorts a stock, he borrows shares from a brokerage and immediately sells them. When the stock goes down in value, the same number of shares are purchased from the market and returned to the brokerage. If the stock does not go down in value (or goes up), then the investor is forced to pay a higher price to obtain the shares he needs to return to the brokerage. In either eventuality, the investor is on the hook for interest payments on the borrowed stock. The longer the borrowing period, the more interest accumulates and the further the stock has to sink in order for the investor to turn a profit.

In investment parlance, when you hear the phrase "going long" or taking a "long position," it refers to a traditional buy-and-hold play, whereby the investor is hoping that the stock will go up in value. "Going short" or taking a "short position" on a stock means the investor wants the stock to lose value within a relatively short period of time.

MY TAKE

ON SHORT SELLING: Short selling is a speculative practice and a much more difficult game than long-term, buy-and-hold investing. If you decide to pursue short selling as part of your investment strategy, your research should be thorough and convincing. Not only are short sellers in a leveraged position, requiring the payment of interest, but their loss potential is unlimited.

Penny Stocks

A penny stock, according to the SEC, is a stock that trades for less than $5 per share. This threshold is the easiest, though perhaps not the most precise, method by which to identify a penny stock. Some investors say that $1 per share is a more appropriate threshold. Penny stocks have a reputation for being exceptionally volatile with much lower liquidity than more conventional stocks. Penny stocks are traded on ***over-the-counter (OTC) markets***. These markets are subject to much less regulation and much lower standards than traditional public exchanges. OTC markets are not centralized exchanges but merely networks of dealers trafficking in exotic and higher-risk securities (like penny stocks). Many of the stock evaluation practices we have covered in this book cannot be reliably applied to penny stocks. Companies that trade their equity shares in OTC markets, for example, are not required to file financial reports with the SEC. They are not even required to be profitable.

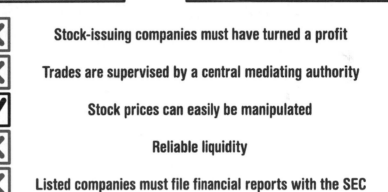

fig. 41

Over the Counter (OTC) Markets	VS.	Traditional Public Exchanges (NYSE, NASDAQ, etc.)
✗	Stock-issuing companies must have turned a profit	✓
✗	Trades are supervised by a central mediating authority	✓
✓	Stock prices can easily be manipulated	✗
✗	Reliable liquidity	✓
✗	Listed companies must file financial reports with the SEC	✓

The appeal of penny stocks trading is rooted in stories of phenomenal returns on investment.

> In 1995, Monster Beverage Corporation, makers of the famous Monster energy drink, was trading at 69 cents per share. Today, Monster (MNST) is on the Nasdaq, trading at $44 per share. That is a return of 6,275 percent.

These rare stories, in addition to the lower costs, make penny stock trading attractive for certain types of investors. For a more thorough exploration of penny stock investing, check out ClydeBank Finance's *Penny Stock Trading QuickStart Guide*.

Forex

Forex stands for "foreign exchange" and refers to the exchanging of one currency for another. The Forex "marketplace" is much more than just another venue for investors and speculators. It is also a critical tool for global business.

Currency exchanges are crucial for international trade, outsourcing, and tourism. The amount of value that changes hands in the Forex market surpasses that of all other trading markets. Every day over four trillion dollars' worth of currency is exchanged. By comparison, $169 billion is traded daily on the New York Stock Exchange.

The Forex trading markets include the spot market, the forward market, and the futures market. The spot market, also known as the physical market or cash market, is where foreign currencies can be exchanged instantly for other currencies. When you leave the airport at an international destination and stop at the currency exchange market to pick up denominations in the local currency, you are trading on the spot market. If you visit your bank before international travel to stock up on foreign money, this transaction likewise occurs on the spot market. The forward and futures Forex markets are similar in that they involve an agreement to purchase a foreign currency at a future date.

Forward contracts are usually negotiated with a bank, and the trades are made over the counter. A price (or exchange rate) is set and the currency is scheduled to be delivered at a specified date. Forex traders and international businesses may use forward markets to hedge against inflation. Typically, a forward contract for a foreign currency is set to be fulfilled one month, three months, or one year after the agreed-upon rate is established. If a currency's forward rate (the price of the currency for future delivery) is higher than its spot rate (current price), then it is said to be selling at a premium. If the forward rate is lower than the spot rate, it is said to be selling at a discount.

Forex trading on the futures market involves the buying and selling of "futures contracts" which oblige the purchasing or selling of a foreign currency at a specific rate. Futures contracts are different from forward contracts because they can be bought and sold multiple times in a public exchange. Forward contracts, by contrast, are privately negotiated and are not typically traded in a secondary market.

The value of forward contracts and futures contracts are determined by market supply and demand. By studying the price of forward and futures contracts you can get an idea of how investors feel a currency's value will change over time.

Some governments do not always allow their currency's value to be determined by the open market, but instead artificially dictate the value of their currency by basing it on (or "pegging it to") the value of another country's currency.

Commodities Futures

The idea of trading commodities futures has its roots in the agriculture industry. Farmers wishing to protect themselves from market volatility would enter into forward contracts with buyers that guaranteed the sale of a certain quantity of agricultural products at a certain time and at a certain price. The modern-day commodities futures market is something of a thrilling playground for traders who are up for a wild ride. When a trader purchases a futures contract, he does not usually intend to actually deliver or purchase the underlying assets. Instead, he aims to enter into an "offsetting contract" that will hopefully result in a profit.

I agree to purchase 500 barrels of oil at the end of a three-month period. The futures price for oil is $50 per barrel. The contract guarantees my right to purchase at $50 per barrel at the end of three months' time, even if the spot price (current price) after three months is higher. If, two months into my futures contract, the price of oil goes up to $60 per barrel, then my contract will be worth more. If I am afraid the price could go back down again before the contract's expiration, I may choose to exit my position by way of an offsetting contract. In this case, my offsetting contract would oblige me to sell 500 barrels of oil the next month (coinciding with the end of my original contract's three-month term). Since the price of the underlying commodity (oil) has increased, the futures price will be higher as well. The new contract, the one that I am selling, will be worth more than the contract I originally bought.

The value of a futures contract is synonymous with the total obligation entailed. In the previous example, my original oil futures contract, which obliged the purchase of 500 barrels for $50 per barrel, could be said to have a value of $25,000. However, when purchasing the contract, I will *not* be asked to fork over the contract's total value. Futures contracts are highly leveraged—meaning a small amount of money is used to control a much larger financial position. You can usually buy or sell a futures contract by putting down a "good faith deposit," which is somewhere around 10 percent of the total contract value. A standard good faith deposit for our oil futures contract would cost us $2,500 (10 percent of $25,000). When the price of oil goes up in the second month to $60 per barrel, the futures contract is now worth $30,000. If we decide to go ahead and exit the position by selling the offsetting contract, the $5,000 profit will be added to our brokerage account. Conversely, if the price of oil goes down, then we may lose not only lose our initial $2,500 investment, but may also be required to add more funds to our brokerage account to offset the loss.

Brokerages that deal in futures require traders to maintain a specific minimum balance, called a "maintenance margin." This balance is used as a buffer to offset losses. If the value of an account drops below the maintenance margin, it must be replenished before any new trades can take place.

You can track the performance of your futures positions on a daily basis simply by tracking the cash value of your brokerage account. Futures exchanges use clearinghouses to move money in and out of customer accounts at the end of each trading day to reflect the current values of a customer's contracts.

The allure of futures trading is the potential for big and fast returns. As with all market opportunities of this nature, however, a congruent level of risk accompanies the chance for reward.

Chapter Recap

» Trading is distinct from investing, often involving greater risk and reward potential.

» Options trading involves the buying and selling of contracts that guarantee the purchase of stock at a future time at a specified price.

» Short selling and buying stocks on margin are higher-risk stock market plays that involve taking stock or money on loan from a brokerage.

» Penny stocks are highly volatile, less liquid, and less regulated than standard securities, but the lure of massive returns on small investments keeps the penny stock market a favorite among thrill-seeking traders.

» The Forex (foreign exchange) market is a tool for global business and a haven for currency speculators.

» Commodities futures markets facilitate the trade of highly leveraged, high-risk contracts that oblige the purchase or sale of certain goods at a specific price at a specific time.

| 7 |
Investment Psychology

Chapter Overview
» Timing the Market
» Trends and Bubbles
» 52-Week Highs and Lows

The market can remain irrational longer than you can remain solvent.
—JOHN MAYNARD KEYNES

As a nonprofessional investor, you have a notable advantage over big fund managers and other financial pros. Take the typical hedge fund manager, for instance. She may be a total genius who knows her way around the market like she knows the back of her hand. But she has some major headwinds blowing her way. She is under constant pressure to show her investors that she can routinely produce big returns. She does not have the luxury of time. If she wants to keep her job she has to post gains. She cannot post a series of losses or less than formidable growth in a bullish market. To achieve the growth her customers demand she has to make a lot of moves. She will move in and out of positions very rapidly. She will buy options contracts. She will take short positions. All this movement has expense, such as broker commissions, slippage, and the other costs of doing business. She is being paid, likely very well, and in order for her to keep her customers she has to justify her cut. Otherwise, why would an investor choose to invest in a hedge fund when he could do just as well or better in a non-actively managed investment vehicle like an ETF?

The huge advantage you have as an amateur investor is that you are under no such pressure. You do not need to incur the expense of making trades every day, or every week for that matter. You can take a look at your portfolio's performance every quarter or so, rebalance it maybe once or twice a year, and you are likely to be A-OK. You do not need to take big risks in order to outpace the market. All you need to do is stay patient and on course with a well-thought-out plan and a disciplined approach.

As a long-term investor, you really are your own worst enemy. Erratic behavior, personal attachments to investments, and other psychological faux pas can drag down the value of your portfolio. In this chapter we will review the psychological virtues and vices of investing.

The Seduction of Market Timing

Given the availability of email alerts and stop-loss orders, it would appear that timing the market—selling off securities in anticipation of an oncoming down market—would be a worthwhile endeavor. Some investors practice the 25% rule. This unofficial, try-it-at-your-own-risk rule states that if a stock goes down by 25% from the highest point it has attained since you bought it, then you should sell it off. Some investors attempt to apply this and similarly arbitrary rules to all holdings in their portfolios. If the total value of their portfolio starts to go down, they hurry to liquidate their assets in hopes of avoiding the brunt of the crash. They must also take it upon themselves to decide when it is safe to reenter the market. Picking just the right times to leave and come back is a lot more difficult than it might seem. In fact, data shows that this approach will almost always leave the investor returns that underperform the market in the long run.

In order to profit significantly from market timing, you have to make two correct predictions.

1. You have to correctly predict an oncoming bear market and sell off your equity positions before the decline.
2. You have to correctly predict an oncoming bull market and buy back into your positions before stocks go back up.

Figure 42 shows the stark contrast between the payoff to be expected from one's attempts at timing the market and the execution of a diligent asset allocation strategy. Our impulse to try to time the market may seem as if it could make all the difference to the success or failure of our investments, but in reality, "getting in at the right time," over the long run, only moves the needle by a tick. Long-term success is built by defining and adhering to a disciplined investment plan.

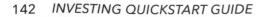

Our fully customizable asset allocation spreadsheet, along with all other digital companion iles to the *Investing QuickStart Guide*, can be accessed for free at: **www.clydebankmedia.com/investing-assets**

Importance of Asset Allocation

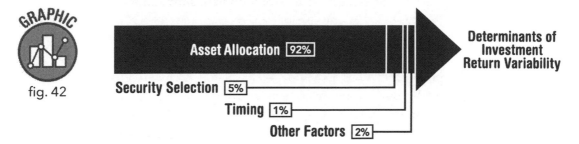

GRAPHIC

fig. 42

Asset Allocation [92%]

Security Selection [5%]

Timing [1%]

Other Factors [2%]

Determinants of
Investment
Return Variability

Given what we know about how bad market crashes can be, selling everything off when it appears that the tides are turning might intuitively seem like a good move. What is easy to ignore, however, is the fact that the market continues to move up and down, often significantly, throughout both bear and bull markets. If you are wrong about the way the market is moving during any given stretch of activity, and you act on your instincts, you will most likely lose money.

To demonstrate the loss potential of overzealous attempts at market timing, The Vanguard Group tracked the performance of a hypothetical $10,000 market index investment from 1988 to 2013. Parameters were set whereby the investment would be pulled out of the market whenever the balance dropped by 25 percent. The investment would reenter the market as soon as the market rose again by 15 percent. The idea here was to simulate what would happen when an investor jumped ship whenever things appeared to be going badly and only reinvested when things appeared peachy keen (exactly what Warren Buffett tells us not to do). The result was that the investment over time performed much more poorly relative to the market, about 36 percent worse over a 26-year period.[55]

The temptation of market timing is a particularly significant psychological hurdle for a lot of investors. Who among us has not looked back over stock and index performance charts during the 2008 financial crisis and fantasized about selling off everything right before the crash, then investing by the boat load when the markets were at rock bottom? It seems so simple! It's not.

Returning to the concept of the "eternal investing conundrum" from chapter 4—market behavior can be explained in retrospect but cannot be reliably predicted. The ability to chart, graph, and explain historical market movement makes it very difficult psychologically to accept the reality that we do not know where the market is headed at any given moment. We are just as likely to guess incorrectly as we are to guess correctly. And in order for any significant payoff to be possible, we would have to guess correctly several times over.

Stocks Are Not Children

Becoming overly attached to certain investments can lead to big mistakes. We tend to treat our portfolio's top performers the same way we treat our favorite children. They are the apple of our eye, and all we ask for is the chance to watch them continue to grow and flourish. This mentality can be counterproductive, if not disastrous. When a stock grows, that is great, but it should not be allowed to grow to such an extent that it offsets your portfolio's balance. If you are maintaining a portfolio of 50% stocks, 40% bonds, 7% real estate, and 3% cash, and a few of your stocks begin performing really well, so much so that stocks move from 50% to 55% of your total asset allocation, then you should consider selling off some of your stocks so you can reinvest in other asset classes and rebalance. Similarly, within your stock portfolio specifically, if you have decided on an allocation of 20% tech stocks, 30% materials, 25% medical, and 25% financial, then you should strive to maintain this allocation. If the value of your tech stocks surpasses that of your other stocks, that is great, but consider selling off some shares and investing in other sectors to maintain your allocation ratio.

In the world of investing, intuition is often the enemy of wisdom. When you see your tech stocks hitting 52-week highs, it may be tempting to let it all ride, or even buy more shares of tech stocks. This may not be wise. The more you fail to sustain diversity, the more exposed you are to risks. What if a market correction sends the tech sector into a downward spiral, as it did in 2001 following the tech bubble? What if a large portion of the growth in tech turns out, again, to be more the result of hype than of sound evaluation? By allowing this sector to dominate your portfolio you expose yourself to additional risk. Never be afraid to sell your high performers.

Another form of attachment that can be counterproductive is refusing to acknowledge your mistake after succumbing to a bad investment. Rather than cut their losses, many investors stubbornly insist that they made the right call even while watching the value of their investment steadily collapse before their eyes. Take note, however—selling an investment at the first sign of trouble is equally problematic. What is important is that you separate your pride and emotion from your most objective evaluation of your position. Everyone who invests makes mistakes. Great investors simply recognize their mistakes faster and do not become emotionally attached to any given investment.

Trends Are Not Always Your Friends

The emergence of a stock bubble, as ill-fated as it may be, is an exciting time to be alive. Everyone's jumping on the bandwagon, making money hand over fist for no good reason. While there is nothing wrong with making money, lots of it, it is important to keep your wits about you in the thick of a good bull market and not get totally swept up in the illusion of limitless cash for the taking. Think about it, though, the stock market cannot keep going up indefinitely. If nothing else, investors will eventually run out of cash to spend on new purchases as stocks continue to trade at higher and higher prices. The companies that are being valued so highly will be under enormous pressure to generate the life-changing products and extraordinary revenues that justify their steep valuations. During the tech bubble of the late '90s and early 2000s, the market posted 20 percent gains with each passing year for five straight years (1995–1999). The Nasdaq (tech index) in particular was going berserk. Some of the P/E ratios on high-priced tech stocks grew to be absurd: 200, 300, some even higher. The ability of these stocks to command such high valuations from the market when they were posting such staggeringly high P/Es is patently absurd in the face of basic economics. Nonetheless, with the pseudo-mysticism of this emerging phenomenon—the internet—in play, many investors no doubt were entertaining the idea that global financial salvation had arrived in the form of tech stocks and technology in general. A never-ending bull market was just one of the many ways in which technology was destined to make our lives perfect. In the midst of this dangerous hypnotism, as investors stared mindlessly into the bright light and promise of the new millennium, the notion of riding to easy riches on the wings of tech and dot com stocks did not seem so far-fetched. These were crazy times.

When you find yourself in a situation where the market's bullishness seems too good to be true, don't get greedy. Continue to rebalance by selling out of positions, sectors, and assets that make up a disproportionately large share of your portfolio.

Sell into strength and buy into weakness.

Resist the temptation of putting more cash than you can afford into the market in an effort to ride the trend as far as it can take you. It will be difficult psychologically to know when to pull back out, even after you have made significant gains. And then of course there is always the possibility that you could take losses you are not prepared to take should the market decide to turn on you. A better approach may be to ease into a diverse portfolio of stocks, ETFs, or mutual funds. Don't beat yourself up about missed opportunities, money you could have invested that would have generated huge returns. There are always going to be woulda/coulda/shoulda scenarios in investing. You just have to learn to live with them.

MY TAKE

ON MARKET TRENDS: As a long-term "buy-and-hold" investor, I am not particularly interested in trends. I am happy leaving most of the technical analysis to the traders. The one trend that I *do* watch is the Fed's action on short-term interest rates. When the Fed rates go higher and longer-term treasuries do not respond in kind, but stagnate instead, flattening the yield curve (see chapter 1), that is when I begin to worry about the prospect of an oncoming recession.

Avoid Fast Decisions

Good investors act not on impulse but on sound judgment. It is tempting to take a "hot tip" that you hear about from a buddy at the bank, because you want to believe that you have an inside track. You want to believe you know something the market does not know. Not to say that you don't, but it is important to learn how to separate actual truth from what you would like to be true. A good way to safeguard against mistakes of impulsive buying or selling is to slow down your investment decision-making process. Do not make a decision based simply on a stock's past performance. Give yourself some time to conduct your fundamental analysis on any security under consideration for admittance into your portfolio. Evaluate the competitors as well. Get a sense of the P/E ratios in the sector and whether the stock you are considering is "cheap." Know how much you can expect in the way of dividend payments, and assess how likely it is that these dividends will be scaled down or increased. Take some time to look over the company's balance sheet. If the balance sheet is in distress, consider how long it might take to recover. Also consider worst-case scenarios. Define a goal for your investment and be realistic about it. Think about your exit strategy, too. Is there a certain level of stagnation or loss you are not willing to tolerate from the investment?

These decisions take longer than a few hours. In the meantime, you may be tempted to agonize over the fact that the stock's gone up by 3 percent while you have been deliberating. Don't let it bother you. Stick to your process and execute with confidence, and only after you are ready.

The Psychological Impact of 52-Week Highs & Lows

Stocks tend to create psychological floors and ceilings for themselves. On many occasions, these limits are built around the 52-week price highs and lows that are widely publicized in financial media. A stock's 52-week low creates a psychological ceiling. When a stock approaches its 52-week low, a lot of investors, assuming that it will not drop any lower, buy the stock. The surge in demand can turn the perception of the price ceiling into reality, and the stock can bounce back on a wave of new buyers. Technical analysts refer to this phenomenon as a "price support." The opposite of a price support is known as a "price resistance." A price resistance seemingly prevents a stock from rising past a certain point. Just as 52-week lows can create psychologically driven price supports, 52-week highs can create psychologically driven price resistance, with investors forming an impression that a stock at its 52-week high point is not likely to go any higher. Many of them sell the stock, driving the price down and psychologically reinforcing the story of the price resistance point.

Chapter Recap

» Discipline and steadiness are key attributes of healthy investment psychology.

» Value a balanced portfolio over any one high-performing stock.

» The movement of a stock's price can be limited by 52-week highs and lows that create psychologically reinforced maximums and minimums.

| 8 |
Beyond Profit
Ethics & Social Responsibility through Investing

Behind every stock is a company. Find out what it's doing.
— PETER LYNCH

We have all heard of C corporations and S corporations, but did you know that there are also B corporations? The B corporation, or "benefit corporation," is a relatively new form of for-profit legal entity. Unlike other corporate legal structures that encourage corporate executives to act in the interests of maximizing profit, B corporation structures oblige executives to also give ample consideration to the corporation's impact on the environment, the community, and society as a whole, in addition to profit. B corporations extend corporate responsibility beyond the simple welfare of the shareholder. Companies benefit from society on several fronts. Without public education, there would be no workforce available for companies to hire out of. Without infrastructure, companies would not be able to ship their goods over highways and rail lines. Without the legal system, companies would not be able collect on debts owed to them. The idea behind socially responsible investing is that companies should act as good corporate citizens and behave in ways that protect and benefit the general welfare as well as their shareholders.[56]

But don't get the wrong idea. B corporations are not charities. In fact, they often attract powerful, intelligent, charismatic personalities to their C-level executive positions, and many of them are quite proficient at turning healthy profits. Sir Richard Branson launched the "B Team" in 2013, an organization dedicated to leveraging the power of business toward social welfare and environmental concerns. In the inaugural press release for the B Team, Branson wrote, "It shouldn't just be left to politicians and community organizations to tackle the world's problems—businesses should help, too."[57] In 2014, Brazilian cosmetics giant Natura became the first publicly traded B corporation.[58]

For those who know where to look, there are abundant opportunities to make socially and environmentally conscious investment decisions. You may find these opportunities in B corporations, alternative energy companies, bonds for projects or municipalities you support, or elsewhere. Perhaps you are shopping for a REIT but would rather not invest in private prisons. Or maybe you want to weed out of your portfolio investments in companies that source labor from countries with weak worker protections. Socially and environmentally conscious investing can help you feel an added sense of pride in your investment decisions. The ability to feel good about where and how your money is put to work, combined with the gain of strong returns, is an ideal and yet attainable state. In this chapter we will discuss how to incorporate the causes you care about into your investment decisions.

Why You Do Not Need to Sacrifice Profit

Ethical investing does not have to come at the expense of profitability. You can and you should have both. In fact, if you support the impact a company's making on the community, the environment, what have you, then you should want assurance that the company is positioned to grow and succeed. What good is accomplished by investing in a company with an amazing social/environmental justice track record when that company is unable to sustain itself financially? A company cannot affect, influence, or model positive change if it cannot operate.

The good news is that it is not terribly difficult to find investment opportunities that meet your ethical criteria and are also poised to thrive. The best approach to this type of investing involves adding an additional layer to your investment evaluation routine. Perhaps included with your fundamental analysis of the investment, you investigate the company's environmental and social impacts and its corporate responsibility reports (aka corporate sustainability reports). If a company is selling overpriced drugs or unhealthy food, promoting rampant deforestation, sourcing labor from countries that permit horrid working conditions, not taking adequate responsibility for its byproducts or pollutants, endangering the health of low-income communities, or any other ethical or moral barrier about which you are passionate, immediately exclude that company.

Various mutual fund companies offer prescreened funds with certain companies or industries filtered out based on moral or ethical criteria. For example, Dimensional Fund Advisors has a lineup of socially responsible funds that screen out companies whose products and practices include, factory farming, child labor, and even for-profit healthcare.

There are plenty of investment opportunities on the market to choose from. Why bother with investments that are out of sync with your values? By the same token, if during your fundamental analysis you come across companies that promote social welfare or responsibility to the environment, that donate generously to worthy charities, that treat their labor force fairly, and that are otherwise admirable corporate citizens, mark those investments for further follow-up. If they pass the other tests of your fundamental analysis—healthy balance sheet, competent leadership, fair P/E ratio, etc.—then you may be looking at a great investment opportunity. When you use ethical investing to narrow down the pool of available opportunities, it can make your evaluation process easier, not more difficult.

A word of warning: do not rely only on a company's self-issued documents and reports when assessing their credibility as ethical corporate actors. On many occasions, the issuing of corporate sustainability reports and the commissioning of socially responsible endeavors are undertaken as a kind of penance for recent breaches in ethics. Be sure to evaluate the reporting of impartial third-party sources alongside a company's own self-reported info.

SRI Screening Services

While fund companies often present their own assortment of self-proclaimed ethical and socially responsible funds, there are also several third-party resources you can turn to when pursuing SRI (socially responsible investment). To name a few,

» *YourSRI.com* – focuses on environmental, social, and governance (ESG) and carbon or greenhouse gas emissions (GHG) issues.

» *MichaelBluejay.com* – an SRI blog that focuses on environmental protection and food and nutrition issues.

» *USSIF.org* – The Forum for Sustainable and Responsible Investment is a nonprofit that publishes reports and comprehensive third-party rating charts for major SRI funds.

The Domini 400 Social Index

This index was created in part by a stockbroker named Amy Domini. Ms. Domini is the author of the book *Ethical Investing*, which probes the available compatibilities between profitability and investing for the social good. Working in concert with her partners, Domini created a new index in 1989, the Domini 400 Social Index, which is a tool for investors who seek more than simply maximal profit. The eligibility of companies included on the index was determined by their adherence to various ethical standards, such as labor relations, safety, community involvement, and environmental conscientiousness. The index automatically excludes companies that deal in tobacco, alcohol, gambling, nuclear power, and firearms.

Though several stocks that comprise the Domini 400 are also on the S&P 500 index, the Domini has an enviable history of regularly outperforming the S&P 500 index.[59] Choosing stocks from the Domini 400 is a good idea for socially conscious investors looking to put their money into blue chips. The companies comprising this index are mainly large-caps.

NOTE

The Domini 400 Social Index is now known as the MSCI KLD 400 Social Index.

The Global 100

Another great way to scout out social difference-makers is by perusing companies recently recognized by the annual Global 100. Every year, during the World Economic Forum in Davos, Switzerland, business and political leaders gather to discuss the global economy and choose 100 companies from around the world who best exemplify commitment to social responsibility and ethics. In 2017, four companies from the United States were in the top 25: the pharmaceutical company Allergan PLC (traded on the NYSE as AGN); McCormick & Co. (MKC), which specializes in food products; Johnson & Johnson (JNJ), specializing in pharmaceuticals; and the communications company Cisco Systems Inc. (CSCO). At the top of the 2017 list was the German industrial company Siemens (SIEGY). In 2016 the US soft drink company Coca-Cola appeared at number 13 on the list.

The Global 100 can be a good resource for kick-starting your search for the best ethical investments. Since there are publicly traded companies from all over the world represented in the listing, you can find worthy international investments here as well. Be forewarned, however, that the evaluation process of the Global 100 does not discriminate against companies that are involved with defense or alcohol. If these are major sticking points for you, then perhaps you will want to begin your search elsewhere.

Use Institutional Investors as a Guiding Light

Institutions that invest can act as guiding lights for socially and environmentally conscious investors. Certain foundations make investments that are financially prudent yet heavily influenced by their commitment to various causes. Foundations, like corporations, have stakeholders, known as beneficiaries. And like companies have executives, foundations have trustees. The trustees have a fiduciary responsibility to the beneficiaries. Trustees are obligated to investigate, analyze, and discern—on behalf of the foundation—the most worthy *and* the most financially viable investment opportunities.

Pension funds are another example of entities that, though obliged to seek positive returns for their stakeholders, also factor in social impact when assessing investment choices. Pension fund investors (pensioners) can influence how fund managers steer their investments and can encourage ethical choices. Religious organizations that employ people will often maintain pension funds, many of which are managed with socially conscientious objectives. But even religious organizations are legally required to make decisions on the basis of highest possible performance. The point being, if you look into the trading activity and portfolios of certain pension funds, you will find examples of investments that, though geared toward profit, are infused with ethical sensitivity. There are various ways of accessing information on the portfolio components of pension funds. The Archdiocese of Los Angeles, for example, maintains a fund for its employees and offers information about the fund via a toll-free phone number.

There are also various nonprofit organizations, such as Sir Richard Branson's aforementioned B Team and the Carbon Tracker Initiative, that make it their business to help align capitalist activity with social and environmental causes. The Carbon Tracker Initiative, for example, pursues action to encourage business behavior that acknowledges and responds to climate change concerns. Among other endeavors, this organization reaches out to pension fund beneficiaries and encourages them to demand that their fund divest out of "bad companies" and invest instead in "the good ones."

Certain pension funds, such as Britain's NEST (National Employment Savings Trust), were explicitly set up to provide an investment option for the ethically conscious investor. Funds like these aim to save employees the trouble of investigating their investment options or lobbying their pension fund to adopt more ethically engaged investment activity.

Ethical Mutual Funds

Given the widespread interest in ethical investing, there are several mutual funds tailored to ethical investors. Choosing to use a mutual fund that you trust will save you the trouble of researching a multitude of prospective companies. Nonetheless, you should always research mutual funds before you buy them. A beautifully written mission statement does not guarantee that the company or mutual fund is living up to their professed standards.

A "socially responsible" fund called Pax World Management Corp. was fined in 2008 for investing in companies that fell outside of its stated criteria. The Securities and Exchange Commission deemed that this violated the rights of the fund's shareholders. In particular, Pax had pledged not to invest in companies tied to gambling or tobacco. It had also pledged not to invest in companies that had more than 5 percent of their revenue coming from defense contracts. During the investigation it became apparent that 8 percent of Pax's investments from 2001 to 2005 had not been properly screened to ensure compliance with the fund's stated standards.[60]

There are a lot of mutual funds out there vying for the attention of socially and ethically minded investors. Let's take a closer look at a few of them:

> **The Domini Funds** – Remember Amy Domini? She had the idea of creating an index that focused on large-cap companies that were doing right by the environment and the people. Well, her company has also created six mutual funds for socially conscious investors.

> **Dimensional Fund Advisors** – Dimensional offers about a dozen socially and ethically minded funds. Dimensional's funds rely heavily on the Fama/French investment model, a strategy we have visited and revisited throughout this text.

Dimensional's funds are "institutional class investments," meaning that they are only offered through financial advisors, albeit with very low expense ratios.

> **Ariel Investments** – Ariel is a wealth management company that manages multiple mutual funds, as well as pensions and endowments. They pride themselves on avoiding investments in tobacco, handguns, and nuclear power while favoring investments in companies that have admirable reputations with regard to labor and the environment. Three of Ariel's mutual fund options are no-load funds, meaning you do not have to pay commission to a salesperson to invest. They tend to focus on companies that have competitive

P/E ratios and other healthy value indicators rather than growth indicators (value versus growth investing is discussed in chapter 4).

» **The Timothy Plan** – Timothy Plan mutual funds stay away from companies it deems contrary to its traditionalist Christian values. You will not find investments in alcohol, tobacco, or pornography in Timothy Plan's collection of mutual funds, nor will you find investments that support benefits for gay marriages and partnerships.

» **Walden Social Equity** – The Walden Social Equity Fund, like many others in the social/ethical sphere, avoids tobacco, alcohol, pornography, and military contractors. It focuses strongly on community relations and workplace conditions.

» **Calvert** – If you are looking for a wide variety of responsible investment options, Calvert has some 28 funds available from which to choose. Calvert is one of the oldest names in socially responsible investing. Their emphases include environmental sustainability, resource efficiency, equitable society, human rights, and accountable corporate governance with an emphasis on transparency.

Corporate governance is discussed in detail in chapter 4.

Ethical ETFs

In chapter 3, we discussed how ETFs are distinct from mutual funds in that they are bought and sold continuously throughout the trading day, just like stocks.

With the growing popularity of ethical investments, many ethical, socially responsible ETFs have been brought to the market. The iShares family (managed by BlackRock) of ethically tailored ETFs is heavily weighted in largecap stocks that have acquired strong reputations for ethical behavior. Among the companies included, you will find Coca-Cola, Alphabet Inc. (Google), Verizon Communications Inc., Microsoft, and Cisco Systems.

Another notable among iShares' ethical ETFs is the iShares MSCI ACWI Low Carbon Target, comprised of large- and mid-cap stocks from both developed and emerging markets. This ETF selects companies that have a lower-than-average carbon footprint.

Another big splash-maker in ethical ETFs is the SPDR S&P 500 Fossil Fuel Free ETF (SPYX). SPYX is an environmentally conscious spin-off of the SPDR S&P 500 ETF Trust SPY, the world's first and largest ETF. SPYX is basically SPY without the fossil fuel companies.

Other major players in ethical ETFs include Barclays, Nushares, and OppenheimerFunds. For PR purposes, brokerages are quite eager to promote their socially responsible/ethical funds and ETFs. For those looking to base their investment decisions on a moral baseline, it should be quite easy to create a short list of prospects.

A Word of Warning about Ethical Investing

For investors, falling in love with a stock or security is always a bad idea, whether it is due to a period of lucrative returns or to a beautifully crafted company mission statement that speaks to cherished values. The risk of investing on the basis of emotion can be exceptionally high with regard to ethical investing.

Ethical investing is not the same as giving to charity.

If your objective is to put your money in a position where it can do the greatest amount of good for the greatest number of people, then spend your energies researching the balance sheets, governance, and mission statements of not-for-profit, charitable institutions.

An ethical investor seeks to invest in securities that can sustain themselves financially and at the same time avoid irresponsible activity and promote the general welfare of the planet and its many inhabitants.

Chapter Recap

» You can invest ethically without diminishing your returns.

» There are several mutual funds and certain ETFs that offer diversified ethical investment opportunities.

» Corporate responsibility reports, sustainability reports, and mission statements can be helpful, but they do not always reveal a company's complete track record in ethics and social responsibility.

| 9 |
Investing Your Way to Financial Freedom

Chapter Overview
» Planning for Financial Freedom
» Early Retirement
» The FIRE Community

Security depends not so much upon how much you have as upon how much you can do without.

—JOSEPH WOOD KRUTCH

An average 5 percent annual return on your investments is certainly not unrealistic. Now, imagine if you could reliably return 5 percent on two million dollars. You would have $100,000 (before tax) in investment returns coming in every year, so long as your principal balance was at least $2,000,000, and so long as the dividends you were receiving remained unchanged by the companies in which you invested. For many individuals, particularly those who value their time more than they value acquiring ever greater thresholds of wealth, $100,000 a year is a perfectly reasonable income. Financial freedom, also known as financial independence, is the ability to generate livable income without having to actively work. It is truly a dream lifestyle and a growing movement, complete with its own online community[61] and semi-secret acronym—financial independents refer to themselves as the "FIRE'd." FIRE stands for "financially independent, retiring early."

Living Below Your Means

One of the recurrent points of emphasis throughout this text is the importance of continually making out-of-pocket contributions to your investment portfolio. Beyond all of the many strategies, analyses, market uncertainties, and other factors that influence the performance of your investments, the act of making continual contributions (saving)—and beginning to do so as early in life as possible—clearly has the biggest across-the-board impact on the growth of your investments over time. For those seeking to achieve "FIRE" status, the emphasis on saving and regularly contributing new capital to your investments is even more paramount. Many people attain financial independence without earning extremely high incomes during their working years. Having a very high income is certainly helpful, but not essential.

The biggest obstacle to financial freedom is not income so much as spending. As we earn more, we have a tendency to spend more. Those who have had success attaining financial freedom are those who have mastered the art of earning a lot more than they spend. For most individuals who are serious about their pursuit of financial freedom, allocating about 50 percent of their income to investments is the proper, albeit rigorous, threshold required. Such an allocation may require you to live in an efficiency apartment at a time when you could afford a nice condo, or you may have to drive a used car when you could easily finance something new. What is even better is to forgo having a car altogether and to commute by walking, cycling, or taking public transit. You have to live below your means, and this may require a bit of psychological hurdle-jumping. Brace yourself to stand by while your peers purchase homes and cars and go on expensive vacations. Keep your eyes on the prize.

Some Americans in their pursuit of financial freedom choose to move to the South, the Midwest, or the Mountain States in pursuit of a lower cost of living. Others may choose to expatriate themselves by moving on a more or less permanent basis to a part of the world that requires much less in the way of cost of living. Such a move may have to wait until after you formally leave the workforce, but in our ever-more-remote economy, there are more ways than ever to work at a location of your choosing.

In our opening example, we considered a 5 percent annual return on an investment of $2,000,000. If we apply the element of frugality to the equation—let's say we are okay with living on $50,000 in annual income—then we can cut our $2,000,000 investment target by half. A 5 percent return on $1,000,000 will be sufficient to provide a $50,000 annual income, which may afford a pretty decent quality of life, especially if you are living in North Dakota.

You are making a trade-off, and the radically liberating privilege of not having to work is hanging in the balance. If you are ambitious and determined to achieve financial freedom, then it is okay to make some sacrifices to achieve this end.

Investment Strategies for Financial Independence

Most investors in pursuit of financial independence need to save about half of their income, which means that evaluating and deciding how to invest these savings will be very important. While each individual or family pursuing financial freedom chooses a distinct path with distinct objectives, there are a few best practices that may aid in this endeavor. To start with, you can gain great advantage by putting your retirement accounts to work. If your employer offers to match your 401(k) contributions, then it goes without saying that you should allocate at least as much to the 401(k) as will be matched. Withdrawing money out of a 401(k) is not cheap—under normal circumstances you will incur a 10 percent penalty. You do, however, have the option of "borrowing" money from your own 401(k) and paying it back to yourself with interest via payroll deductions. Borrowing from your 401(k) should be considered only as a last resort option, due to the opportunity cost you will incur from not having your investments working for you in the market. After separating from your employer, you can convert your 401(k)—if it makes sense in light of your tax situation—into a Roth IRA account to access more flexible withdrawal options. Roth IRAs, unlike traditional IRAs, do not require you to start withdrawing minimum distributions at age 70½. This flexibility may help you better manage your social security distributions when the time comes, since Roth IRA distributions do not affect the taxability of social security income. In other words, you can take money out, when you want it (not before) and it will not in any way diminish your social security entitlement. Just remember that if you are moving untaxed funds from your recently dismissed employer's 401(k) into a Roth IRA, then you will have to pay taxes that year on the funds you move.

REMEMBER

All money that goes into a Roth IRA is "post-tax" income. You must claim the money as income in the year that you earn it. That is why you are able to withdraw out of a Roth IRA tax-free (after age 59½). Money contributed to traditional 401(k)s and IRAs is "pre-tax" income. You can deduct your contributions from your income, but you will pay tax on the money when you make withdrawals.

NOTE

Some employers offer a "Roth 401(k)," which operates similarly to a Roth IRA for tax purposes. The money you contribute is taxed going in and will not be taxed when you make your withdrawals. If you leave your employer, you can easily roll your Roth 401(k) into a Roth IRA, tax-free.

Growth is, of course, what you are after when building your financial escape hatch. Your portfolio should be well-balanced and should favor stocks. ETFs and low-cost mutual funds are nice, as they are pre-diversified securities with the possibility of substantial growth over time.

One way to track the progress you are making on your early retirement is to decide on a financial "critical mass," a quantity of money that can generate enough reliable return to sustain your financial needs and lifestyle expectations. Once that mass is reached, you can steadily convert some of your growth-oriented stocks into high-dividend-paying stocks, preferred stocks, bonds, and other more stable investments that offer steadier income. Again, there are so many factors at play that it is impossible to prescribe a one-size-fits-all path to financial independence. Each individual and family will need to do a lot of finely tuned planning. Do you have children who will likely attend college? Are you planning on traveling during your retirement or embarking on any other activities that may require substantial investment? Do you have a backup plan ready to deploy in the event of a major financial disaster? Do you have a cash reserve? Will you or your spouse be able to reenter the workforce if need be?

Trying to plan out so many decades of your financial future may seem daunting. You have no clue how dramatically your interests, aptitudes, and abilities will change in the space between your forties and your seventies. Nonetheless, you should still make a plan, even though it will not be perfect. Create a living budget to account for your expected expenses after you "retire." Do multiple projections that incorporate several different market eventualities. You need contingencies in place in the event you have less or more money to work with than you had originally anticipated. Should you find yourself "retired" but with fewer funds available than you require, then you may need to reduce your distributions or start working for an income again. If you have more income than you anticipate, then you will need to decide how much of your excess you want to spend and how much you want to reinvest or sock away in a savings account. Again, coming up with a precise roadmap will be impossible as there are too many variables in play. The intent of this front-end planning is not to predict the future but to expose you to a range of potential outcomes, ensuring that you develop an effective and flexible financial independence plan that accommodates your lifestyle and goals.

ON PURSUING FINANCIAL INDEPENDENCE: Based on my personal experience, investors who attain financial independence possess three critical attributes:

1. The discipline to consistently save money
2. Good investment behavior (avoiding market timing and other pitfalls)
3. Good personal budgeting skills

The Purpose Fulfillment Variable

As the saying goes, "Don't retire *from* something, retire *to* something." It is interesting how people who have attained financial freedom often find themselves looking for ways to exert their energies in order to feel fulfilled. Whether through volunteering, helping out family or friends, or even taking odd and random jobs just for the experience, there seems to be an innate drive within the financially independent community toward meaningful pursuits of one kind or another. The anonymous author of the FIRE blog, Our Next Life, goes so far as to proclaim it as essential that you have a clear idea of how you intend to occupy yourself after achieving financial independence [62] (the author of this blog chooses to remain anonymous, as she and her husband plan on retiring sometime this year, at ages 41 and 38, respectively). Apparently, they do not want their plans known by current employers or other interested parties.

As great as it may seem to not have to work, do not make the mistake of seeing it as an end in itself. Financial independents who have nothing with which to occupy themselves are likely to experience a type of occupational empty nest syndrome, which can lead to anxiety and even depression. It is best to identify your personal passions and to plan for an active post-retirement lifestyle.

Chapter Recap

> » With disciplined frugality and careful planning, financial freedom can be attained even by those with moderate incomes.

> » Retiring early means having more years of retirement to plan for; be sure to consider the unexpected and plan for contingencies.

> » The pursuit of financial independence should be inspired by a call to a passion, not just by a motivation not to work.

Conclusion

A goal without a plan is just a wish.

– ANTOINE DE SAINT-EXUPÉRY

Good financial advisors (and good financial books) do not predict the market. They prepare you for it. By studying and understanding the mechanics of the stock market, you are better equipped to avoid its perils and participate in its rewards. You are not going to lose your cool during a downturn, and you will not let emotional attachment stand in the way of prudent investment choices. You will understand the lay of the land when it comes to seeking help, from robo-advisors to CFPs and everything in between. Investing is always an adventure, marked by uncertainty, hopefulness, fear, surprise delights, and treasure hunting. If you have come this far, then you are already well on your way to experiencing the excitement of the market firsthand. Just remember to keep your wits about you, along with a good sense of humor and humility. You will be fine.

MY TAKE

ON GENERAL FINANCIAL PLANNING & WELL-BEING: If you have read and studied this book, then you should now possess a foundation for success in the world of investing. But investing, although a big part of financial planning, is not the only part. Other elements include tax, business, insurance, retirement, and estate planning. It is often hard to make a change in one of these areas without affecting the others. Furthermore, certain decisions you make as an investor may have unintended consequences in other areas of your financial life, consequences of which you may not be aware. Enlisting the services of a CFP® practitioner can help you build and execute coordinated plans that will promote success in all areas of your financial life.

About The Author

Website: www.snowfinancialgroup.com
LinkedIn: www.linkedin.com/in/tedsnow
Twitter: www.twitter.com/tedsnowcfp
Email: tsnow@snowfinancialgroup.com
Phone: 469-522-4056

TED D. SNOW, CFP®, MBA

My roots in the financial services industry started in 1987 when I began working at a well-known investment company based in Boston. Over the next ten years, the best education I received was learning the securities industry by helping customers with mutual fund investing, individual securities trading, and financial planning concepts, all while learning to provide superior customer service. In the last year of my career at this company, I grew uneasy. I had the desire to advise people with much more depth than I was allowed to. I saw too many people making emotional and risky financial decisions because they chose to "do it themselves." They simply didn't know what they didn't know. Coordination of retirement, investments, insurance, business, estate, and taxes was how I could truly help these customers, who were in desperate need of help.

While earning my MBA in financial planning at the University of Dallas, I developed a desire for entrepreneurship and decided it was time to take a huge leap of faith to start my own practice. With no clientele, but armed with industry knowledge and the skill of great customer service, I set out to build a financial planning practice.

After spending eight additional years with independent firms building my practice, I founded Snow Financial Group LLC in 2006 with the purpose of offering true personal service to my clients. We focus on two primary values: first, offering great client service. We keep our client list small to provide clients quick access to me and the staff while cultivating great relationships. Our second value is creating a comfortable and easy atmosphere where people like to come and talk about their financial lives. The industry has changed so much since 1987; however, my passion for these core values has proven to be a successful formula. Snow Financial Group starts with being personal. I feel like the families in my practice are part of my personal family. If you decide to be one of the families we serve at Snow Financial Group, you will experience wealth management like you've never experienced it before: personally.

Disclosure

Securities may be offered through registered representatives of Kestra Investment Services, LLC Member FINRA/SIPC and is not affiliated with any other entity referenced. The opinions expressed in this publication are those of the author and may not necessarily reflect those held by Kestra Investment Services. Kestra Investment Services does not offer legal or tax advice.

About ClydeBank Media

We create simplified educational tools that allow our customers to successfully learn new skills in order to navigate this constantly changing world.

The success of ClydeBank Media's value-driven approach starts with beginner-friendly high-quality information. We work with subject matter experts who are leaders in their fields. These experts are supported by our team of professional researchers, writers, and educators.

Our team at ClydeBank Media works with these industry leaders to break down their wealth of knowledge, their wisdom, and their years of experience into small and concise building blocks. We piece together these building blocks to create a clearly defined learning path that a beginner can follow for successful mastery.

At ClydeBank Media, we see a new world of possibility. Simplified learning doesn't have to be bound by four walls; instead, it's driven by you.

Your world, simplified.™

Glossary

10-K
Annual financial report that is required of publicly traded companies.

10-Q
Quarterly financial report that supplements the 10-K.

Ask price
The stock price at which a market maker can guarantee a transaction for a buyer. Think of an ask price as the amount someone is willing to immediately accept in order to buy a stock.

Bid price
The stock price at which a market maker can guarantee a transaction for a seller. Think of a bid price as the amount someone is willing to immediately accept in order to sell a stock.

Bond
An IOU issued by a government or private enterprise in exchange for cash. Bondholders (buyers) are paid interest at fixed intervals and rates and are repaid the bond's full principal amount at a future maturity date.

Bubble
When the price of stocks or other securities becomes inflated due to herd behavior and overzealous investor confidence not rooted in sound fundamental analysis.

Call option
An options contract that guarantees the option "owner" the right to purchase a stock at a specified price (strike price) before a specified expiration date.

Capital gain
A profit resulting from an investor's ownership in a stock or other investment that has increased in value and can be sold at a price higher than its original purchase price.

Capital structure
The way in which a company secures capital. The issuance of debt (bonds) and equity (stocks) are the primary methods of securing capital.

Corporate governance
The layout and functioning of a corporation's management, including a system of rules, control hierarchies, policies, values, shareholder interests, community, and other factors.

Correlation
The similar response of certain stocks to various outside factors, scored on a range from -1 to +1. Two stocks are perfectly correlated if they have a correlation value of +1. They are perfectly non-correlated if they have a correlation value of -1.

Cost basis
The cost basis for a stock is the original cost of obtaining the stock adjusted for income obtained through the stock, such as dividends, capital distribution, and any income gained from selling options on the stock.

Covered call
When a trader selling a call option owns the requisite shares in the underlying asset and is therefore able to readily produce the shares if the option is "called in."

Debt-to-asset ratio
Also known as "debt ratio," a ratio used to quantify the percentage of a company's assets that are financed by creditors.

Debt-to-equity ratio
A comparative measurement of the claims on a company's value exerted by creditors vs. the claims exerted by equity holders (shareholders).

Deflation
When fewer units of currency have the power to purchase more goods and services. Deflation results from a decline in available money supply.

Derivative
A security that derives its price from the price of other assets. Examples of derivative securities include options and commodities futures contracts.

Dividend
Cash payment issued by a company to its stockholders on a regular basis, usually quarterly.

Due diligence
The mandated inspection of a security by brokerages that must take place before the broker brings the security to market.

Earnings per share (EPS)
Total company profit divided by total outstanding shares.

Efficient market hypothesis (EMH)
The theory that all available information about a stock is reflected in its current price.

Equity
A party's ownership percentage in a business, corporation, or other property.

ETF (exchange traded fund)
ETFs are a pre-diversified, tradable security, but unlike mutual funds, ETF prices can fluctuate throughout the day. ETFs operate on the market in essentially the same manner as a stock.

Expense ratio
An annual fee charged by the managers of mutual funds or ETFs. Expense ratios account for administrative overhead and other fixed costs of managing the fund or ETF.

Foreign tax withholding
Taxes applied to investment income earned by nonresident investors.

Fundamental analysis
The evaluation of core quantitative and qualitative attributes defining the financial vitality of a security's underlying assets. In the case of stocks, the subject of a fundamental analysis would be the corporation or business that is issuing the stock.

Growth investing
Investing on the basis of a great story, inspired by companies that are making big splashes in relevant market sectors. Growth investors are open to investing in companies with higher levels of debt, higher P/E ratios, and lower earnings per share (EPS). Compare with "value investing."

Growth stock
A stock that may not have particularly competitive financials but is eagerly sought by the market nonetheless on the basis of anticipated growth rather than dividend income.

GTC limit order
A limit order that is "good till canceled." A GTC, unlike a regular limit order (see definition below) does not expire at the end of the trading day. GTC limit orders expire only after a specified period of days has elapsed or after the investor cancels them. A 60-day GTC limit order, for example, is good for 60 days or until canceled.

Hedge fund
Speculative, actively managed fund aimed at high-net-worth individuals. Hedge fund managers pursue aggressive growth through the use of derivative securities, short positions, and other forms of complex investment strategies.

Index fund
A mutual fund comprised of stocks that reflect the composition of a specific market index.

Index investing
Investing in a mutual fund or ETF comprised of stocks that reflect the composition of a specific market index.

Inflation
The decline of a currency's purchasing power.

Initial Public Offering (IPO)
The first open-market offering of equity shares in a newly public company.

Leverage
The application of borrowed capital for the purpose of acquiring investments for a greater return potential, albeit with a greater risk. Leverage can enhance returns and exacerbate losses.

Limit order
An order placed to buy or sell a stock if and only if the stock reaches a specified price. Limit orders are distinct from market orders in that there is no guarantee that the transaction will be executed. Unless the limit order is "GTC" (see definition above) it expires at the end of the current trading day.

Liquidity
A measure of how fast a stock or other asset can be turned into cash.

Long position
An investment whereby a return is realized if the purchased security gains value over time.

Long-term capital gain
Profit made from purchasing a security and holding it for at least a year before selling it for a gain. Long-term capital gains are taxed at the capital gains tax rate, which is generally favorable relative to the standard income tax paid on short-term capital gains.

Marketability
The ability to trade a stock or other asset at a given price at a given volume.

Market capitalization
Stock price multiplied by total shares outstanding. Market capitalization is used as a measurement of a company's overall size and total value.

Market correction
A sudden downturn in the market due to inflated stock prices and general overestimations of the market's strength.

Market maker
A firm that publicly quotes stock prices to the public. In order to ensure liquidity, market makers must be willing to buy and sell stock at the prices they quote.

Market order
An order to buy or sell stock whereby the broker commits to an immediate transaction at an available market price. Market orders are used when investors prioritize the immediate execution of a trade over the exact price of a trade.

Mutual fund
A professionally managed investment vehicle divided into shares and powered by investments in stocks, bonds, or other securities, and funded by shareholders.

Mutual fund load
The commission paid to an advisor or broker for researching and selecting a mutual fund on a client's behalf.

NAV (net asset value)
Used to measure the value of a mutual fund. NAV is the aggregate per-share value of all securities that comprise a mutual fund, minus expenses. NAV values do not fluctuate throughout the day like stock values but instead are priced once at the end of each business day to reflect the day's valuation change.

New York Stock Exchange

The largest stock exchange in the world, as determined by the combined total market capitalization values of the securities represented on the exchange.

Normal yield curve

The standard relationship between a bond's term and its yield. In a normal yield curve, the longer the bond's term (the more time allowed to pass before the bond's face value is returned to the investor) the higher its yield.

Over-the-counter (OTC) market

Trading venues that are networks of dealers. OTC markets are subject to fewer standards and regulations compared to centralized exchange markets but tend to be fair in transacting securities trades.

Part B prospectus

A secondary component of a mutual fund's prospectus that often includes important variable expense information and other data not found in the general prospectus. Part B prospectuses are usually not issued automatically. They often must be explicitly requested by the investor.

P/E (price-earnings) ratio

A stock evaluation metric that is calculated by dividing a stock's price by its earnings per share. Stocks with lower P/Es are considered "cheap." Stocks with higher P/Es are considered more expensive.

Prospectus

A report issued on behalf of a mutual fund disclosing the fund's strategy, goals, fixed expenses, and risks.

Put option

An options contract that guarantees the option "owner" the right to sell a stock at a certain price (strike price) before a specified expiration date.

Realized capital gain

When an investor sells out of an investment position at a profit: receiving more cash than what he originally paid to buy into the position. Also known as a "realized gain."

Rebalancing

The investor's periodic portfolio checkup, ensuring that asset ownership is proportioned evenly with no undue risk resulting from an over- or under-abundance of one asset type or another.

REIT (real estate investment trust)

REITs are funds devoted to the acquisition and management of real estate assets for profit. REITs allow investors to own pieces of properties without having to hire a property management company or self-manage.

SEC (Securities & Exchange Commission)

The federal regulatory agency that oversees the buying, selling, and marketing of stocks, bonds, and other financial securities.

Security

A stock, bond, mutual fund, ETF, or other financial instrument that confers financial value to an extent determined by the market's demand.

Settlement date

Regarding the purchase or sale of a stock, the settlement date refers to the date on which the transfer of cash and legal stock ownership actually takes place.

Short position

An investment transaction whereby a gain is realized if the security loses value over time.

Short-term capital gain

Profit made from purchasing a security and then selling it for a gain within a year's time. Short-term capital gains are taxed at your standard income tax rate.

Slippage cost

The difference between an investor's expected price when buying or selling a stock and the actual price paid or received for the stock. Slippage is the result of swift market changes that may transpire between the investor's placement of an order and the broker's execution of that order. Instances of slippage are usually witnessed following the execution of a market or stop-loss order.

Socially responsible investing

The selection of investments on the basis of moral values and/or positive civic, humanitarian, or environmental implications, in addition to financial return potential.

Stock

Equity shares issued by a business or corporation in exchange for capital to further fund business development and growth.

Stock market index

A measurement based on certain attributes of a qualified assortment of stocks. Stock market indexes are used to track the overall performance of various sections of the market. Examples include the Dow Jones Industrial Average, the Nasdaq, and the S&P 500.

Stock split

When a company divides its shares so that each outstanding share is suddenly worth two shares, three shares, or some other multiple. Theoretically, the stock's price will decrease in proportion to the split, but oftentimes the market will try to buoy the stock back toward its pre-split price.

Stop-limit orders

An order to buy or sell a stock in the event that it drops below (or climbs above) a specified price (known as the "stop price"). Stop-limit orders trigger a limit order (see definition) when the stop price is reached.

Stop-loss order

An order to buy or sell a stock in the event that it drops below (or climbs above) a specified price (known as the "stop price"). Stop-loss orders trigger a market order (see definition) when the stop price is reached.

Tax-loss harvesting

Refers to selling a security at a loss in order to offset income and/or capital gains from the sale of other securities.

Technical analysis

Distinct from fundamental analysis, technical analysis is the evaluation of a stock or other security on the basis of its behavior in the market. Technical analysis concentrates on the perceived trends and patterns that affect a stock's price, whereas fundamental analysis is immediately focused on the vitality (financial and otherwise) of the company itself using financial statements and other reported financial data of the company.

Term

A specified period of time that a bondholder must wait until the bond's principal (face value) is returned. The bondholder is paid interest throughout the term. (Also known as "maturity date")

Trading volume

The total quantity of stock shares being traded during a given time interval.

Unrealized capital gain

Also known as an "unrealized gain," an investment position that has appreciated in value and is still being held by the investor. An "unrealized gain" becomes a "realized gain" when the investor sells out of the position in exchange for cash.

Value investing

Investing on the basis of sound financial fundamentals. Value investors invest in companies that consistently turn profits, pay dividends, have low debt, and are undervalued compared to competitors in the same industry.

Value stock

Stock whose valuation will hold up amid the scrutiny of fundamental analysis (see definition above). Value stocks have low P/E ratios, competitive yield, and reasonable debt levels. And they are undervalued compared to competitors in the same industry.

Volatility

The degree to which a stock or other asset's price is subject to fluctuation. Measurements of volatility may also be applied to markets as a whole. Volatility encompasses not only downside market movement but upward movement as well.

Disclosures

CHAPTER 3:

a   The target date is the approximate date when investors plan on withdrawing their money. Generally, the asset allocation of each fund will change on an annual basis with the asset allocation becoming more conservative as the fund nears target retirement date. The principal value of the funds is not guaranteed at any time including at and after the target date.

b   Any guarantee of annuity payments is based on the claims paying ability of the issuing insurance company.

c   Distributions from non-publically traded REITs may be paid from sources of funds other than operational income. These sources may include loans and a return of capital, and they may create tax consequences for the REIT as well as for the investor. A trust's failure to qualify as a REIT may also result in tax consequences for both the REIT and the investor.

CHAPTER 6:

d   **Day Trading Disclosures**

The following disclosures apply specifically to the practice of "day trading," (introduced in Chapter 6 of this book).

Day trading can be extremely risky. Day trading generally is not appropriate for someone of limited resources and limited investment or trading experience and low risk tolerance. You should be prepared to lose all of the funds that you use for day trading. In particular, you should not fund day-trading activities with retirement savings, student loans, second mortgages, emergency funds, funds set aside for purposes such as education or home ownership, or funds required to meet your living expenses. Further, certain evidence indicates that an investment of less than $50,000 will significantly impair the ability of a day trader to make a profit. Of course, an investment of $100,000 or more will in no way guarantee success.

Be cautious of claims of large profits from day trading. You should be wary of advertisements or other statements that emphasize the potential for large profits in day trading. Day trading can also lead to large and immediate financial losses.

Day trading requires knowledge of a firm's operations. You should be familiar with a securities firm's business practices, including the operation of the firm's order execution systems and procedures. Under certain market conditions, you may find it difficult or impossible to liquidate a position quickly at a reasonable price. This can occur, for example, when the market for a stock suddenly drops, or if trading is halted due to recent news events or unusual trading activity. The more volatile a stock is, the greater the likelihood that problems may be encountered in executing a transaction. In addition to normal market risks, you may experience losses due to system failures.

Day trading will generate substantial commissions, even if the per trade cost is low. Day trading involves aggressive trading, and generally you will pay commissions on each trade. The total daily commissions that you pay on your trades will add to your losses or significantly reduce your earnings. For instance, assuming that a trade costs $16 and an average of 29 transactions are conducted per day, an investor would need to generate an annual profit of $111,360 just to cover commission expenses.

Day trading on margin or short selling may result in losses beyond your initial investment. When you day trade with funds borrowed from a firm or someone else, you can lose more than the funds you originally placed at risk. A decline in the value of the securities that are purchased may require you to provide additional funds to the firm to avoid the forced sale of those securities in your account. Short selling as part of your day-trading strategy also may lead to extraordinary losses, because you may have to purchase a stock at a very high price in order to cover a short position.

Potential Registration Requirements. Persons providing investment advice for others or managing securities accounts for others may need to register as either an "Investment Adviser" under the Investment Company Act of 1940 or as a "Broker" or "Dealer" under the Securities Exchange Act of 1934. Such activities may also trigger state registration requirements.

e   ## Options Trading Disclosure

The following disclosure applies specifically to the practice of "options trading," (introduced in Chapter 6 of this book).

Options trading entails significant risk and is not appropriate for all investors. Certain complex options strategies carry additional risk. Before trading options, please read Characteristics and Risks of Standardized Options, published by Options Clearing Corporation (OCC) https://www.theocc.com/. Transaction costs may be significant in multi-leg option strategies, including straddles and strangles, as they involve multiple commission charges.

Supporting documentation for any claims, if applicable, will be furnished upon request. The information in this book, including examples using actual securities and price data, is strictly for illustrative and educational purposes only and is not to be construed as an endorsement or recommendation.

f   The brokerage firm can sell your securities without contacting you. You may be given a due date to cover a margin call but the firm may liquidate assets prior to that due date at their discretion.

g   ## Margin Disclosures

The following disclosures apply specifically to the practice of buying stocks and other securities on margin, (introduced in Chapter 6 of this book).

You can lose more funds than you deposit in the margin account. A decline in the value of securities that are purchased on margin may require you to provide additional funds to the firm that has made the load to avoid the forced sale of those securities or other securities or assets in your account(s).

The firm can force the sale of securities or other assets in your account(s). If the equity in your account falls below the maintenance margin requirements, or the firm's higher "house" requirements, the firm can sell the securities or other assets in any of your accounts held at the firm to cover the margin deficiency. You also will be responsible for any short fall in the account after such a sale.

The firm can sell your securities or other assets without contacting you. Some investors mistakenly believe that a firm must contact them for a margin call to be valid, and that the firm cannot liquidate securities or other assets in their accounts to meet the call unless the firm contacts them first. This is not the case. Most firms will attempt to notify their customers of margin calls, but they are not required to do so. However, even if a firm has contacted a customer and provided a specific date by which the customer can meet a margin call, the firm can still take necessary steps to protect its financial interests, including immediately selling the securities without notice to the customer.

You are not entitled to choose which securities or other assets in your account(s) are liquidated or sold to meet a margin call. Because the securities are collateral for the margin loan, the firm has the right to decide which security to sell in order to protect its interests.

The firm can increase its "house" maintenance margin requirements at any time and is not required to provide you advance written notice. These changes in firm policy often take effect immediately and may result in the issuance of a maintenance margin call. Your failure to satisfy the call may prompt the firm to liquidate or sell securities in your accounts(s).

You are not entitled to an extension of time on a margin call. While an extension of time to meet margin requirements may be available to customers under certain conditions, a customer does not have a right to the extension.

References

INTRODUCTION:

1   Tim McMahon, "Annual Inflation," *InflationData.com*, January 18, 2017, http://www.inflationdata.com/inflation/inflation/AnnualInflation.asp.

2   Mike Jelinek, "The Best High-Interest Savings Accounts Online for 2017," *The Simple Dollar*, February 2, 2018, http://www.thesimpledollar.com/best-high-interest-savings-accounts/.

3   Trent Hamm, "Average Stock Market Return: Where Does 7% Come From," *The Simple Dollar*, March 27, 2016, http://www.thesimpledollar.com/where-does-7-come-from-when-it-comes-to-long-term-stock-returns/.

4   Ted Snow, "The Price of 'Safe," *Snow Financial Group*, http://www.snowfinancialgroup.com/blog/the-price-of-safe.

5   ClydeBank Finance, *Options Trading QuickStart Guide*, (Albany: ClydeBank Media, 2016).

6   ClydeBank Finance, *Penny Stock Trading QuickStart Guide*, (Albany: ClydeBank Media, 2016).

CHAPTER 1:

7   Burton G. Malkiel, *The Random Walk Guide to Investing* (New York, W.W. Norton & Company 2003), 11.

8   "Principle 4: Maintain perspective and long-term discipline," *Advice and Guidance*, Vanguard.com, accessed 4/10/2017.

9   Data derived from Dimensional Fund Advisors LP, "Dimensions of Expected Returns: Historical premiums and returns (annualized): US, Developed ex US, and Emerging Markets," *Performance of Premiums in the Equity Markets*. Dimensional Index data compiled by Dimensional. Fama/French data provided by Fama/French, Presentation, 2016.

10   US Securities and Exchange Commission, "SEC Adopts T+2 Settlement Cycle for Securities Transactions," news release, March 22, 2017, www.sec.gov/news/press-release/2017-68-0.

11   NYSE, (February 21, 2018), Google Finance, stock quote.

CHAPTER 2:

12   The Wall Street Journal, "How to Choose a Financial Planner," Guides/Personal Finance (blog), *The Wall Street Journal*, 2016, http://guides.wsj.com/personal-finance/managing-your-money/how-to-choose-a-financial-planner/.

13   Geoff Williams, "How to Find a Financial Advisor If You're Not Rich," *US News and World Report*, February 26, 2014, http://money.usnews.com/money/personal-finance/financial-advisors/articles/2014/02/26/how-to-find-a-financial-advisor-if-youre-not-rich.

14   Top Ten Reviews, "The Best Online Stock Trading Brokers of 2017," Purch, 2017, http://www.toptenreviews.com/money/investing/best-online-stock-trading-brokers/.

15   Teresa Epperson, Bob Hedges, Uday Singh, Monica Gabel, "Hype vs. Reality: The Coming Waves of 'Robo' Adoption" (from the "Insights from the A.T. Kearney 2015 Robo-Advisory Services Study," June 2015).

16   Arielle O'Shea, "Best Robo-Advisors: 2017 Top Picks," *Nerdwallet*, June 23, 2017, https://www.nerdwallet.com/blog/investing/best-robo-advisors/.

17   Source: http://blog.helpingadvisors.com.

CHAPTER 3:

18   Andy Kiersz, "Here's the Difference Between Someone Who Starts Saving at 25 vs. Someone Who Starts at 35," Your Money (blog), *Business Insider*, March 25, 2014, http://www.businessinsider.com/saving-at-25-vs-saving-at-35-2014-3

19   Jeremy Siegel, *Stocks for the Long Run* (New York: McGraw-Hill, 2014).

20   Source: http://tradinginvestment.com, accessed January 26, 2017.

21   ClydeBank Finance, *Penny Stock Trading QuickStart Guide*, (Albany: ClydeBank Media, 2016).

22   ClydeBank Finance, *Penny Stock Trading QuickStart Guide*.

23   Neither I nor my publisher has any ownership or commissioned interest in PersonalFund.com, but I do use it regularly.

24   Ryan Vlastelica, "SEC kicks the bitcoin ETF approval decision down the road," *MarketWatch*, October 13, 2016, http://www.marketwatch.com/story/sec-kicks-the-bitcoin-etf-approval-decision-down-the-road-2016-10-13.

25   ETFGI, "ETFGI reports ETFs/ETPs listed in the United States gathered record inflows of 279 billion US dollars and assets reached a new high of 2.549 trillion US dollars at the end of 2016," *ETFGI.com*, January 20, 2017, http://etfgi.com/news/detail/newsid/1573.

26   Todd Shriber, "Gen X, Millennials Driving ETF Growth," *Benzinga*, January 24, 2017, https://www.benzinga.com/news/17/01/8936438/gen-x-millennials-driving-etf-growth.

27   Nathaniel Popper, "S.E.C. Rejects Winklevoss Brothers' Bid to Create Bitcoin E.T.F." *New York Times*, March 10, 2017, https://www.nytimes.com/2017/03/10/business/dealbook/winkelvoss-brothers-bid-to-create-a-bitcoin-etf-is-rejected.html.

28   Marco Cipriani, Michael Holscher, Antoine Martin, and Patrick McCabe, "Twenty-Eight Money Market Funds That Could Have Broken the Buck: New Data on Losses during the 2008 Crisis," *Liberty Street Economics*. Federal Reserve Bank of New York, October 09, 2013, http://libertystreeteconomics.newyorkfed.org/2013/10/twenty-eight-money-market-funds-that-could-have-broken-the-buck-new-data-on-losses-during-the-2008-c.html.

29   "Money market breaks the buck, freezes redemptions." *MarketWatch*, Fund Watch, September 17, 2008, http://www.marketwatch.com/story/money-market-fund-breaks-the-buck-freezes-redemptions.

30   Alex Crippen, "Buffett has big lead in bet against hedge funds," Warren Buffett Watch (blog), CNBC, February 6, 2014, http://www.cnbc.com/2014/02/06/buffett-has-big-lead-in-bet-against-hedge-funds.html.

31   These futures are current as of the 2018 tax year but are subject to change year by year.

CHAPTER 4:

32   Peter Coy, "Bill Clinton's drive to increase homeownership went way too far," *Bloomberg*, February 26, 2008, https://www.bloomberg.com/news/articles/2008-02-26/bill-clintons-drive-to-increase-homeownership-went-way-too-far.

33   Malkiel, *The Random Walk Guide to Investing*, 21.

34   James Altucher, *The Forever Portfolio*, (New York: Portfolio 2008), 120.

35   NYSE, (2017, February 2), Google Finance, stock quote.

36   Matthew Frankel, "10 Warren Buffet Quotes That Teach Us About Investing," *The Motley Fool*, July 24, 2016, https://www.fool.com/investing/2016/07/24/10-warren-buffett-quotes-that-teach-us-about-inves.aspx.

37   Altucher, *The Forever Portfolio*, 96.

38   Tony Daltorio, "What Investors Can Learn from Legendary Investor Sir John Templeton," *Investing Answers*, http://www.investinganswers.com/education/famous-investors/what-investors-can-learn-legendary-investor-sir-john-templeton-1103.

39   Altucher, *The Forever Portfolio*, 11.

40   Kate Taylor, "Monopoly: Global Food Supply Controlled By Ten Companies" *Technocracy News & Trends*, April 6, 2017, https://www.technocracy.news/index.php/2017/04/06/monopoly-global-food-supply-controlled-ten-companies/.

41   Martinne Geller, "NESTLE CEO: Warren Buffet just 'pulverized the food industry market,'" *Business Insider*, April 16, 2015, http://www.businessinsider.com/r-nestle-says-taking action-to-keep-top-slot-in-food-industry-2015-4.

42   Bill Vlasic, "G.M., Once a Powerhouse, Pleads for Bailout," *The New York Times,* November 11, 2008, http://www.nytimes.com/2008/11/12/business/12auto.html.

43   Gary Brinson, L. Randolph Hood, & Gilbert Beebower, "Determinants of Portfolio Performance," *Financial Analysts Journal* 42, no. 4 (July-August 1986, Updated 1991): 39, doi: 10.2469/faj.v42.n4.39.

44   Janet Levaux, Emerging Markets Dominate Global GDP, The Portfolio (blog), *ThinkAdvisor*, May 9, 2014, http://www.thinkadvisor.com/2014/05/09/emerging-markets-dominate-global-gdp?slreturn=1488580048.

45   Lance Roberts, "Dalbar: Why Investors Suck and Tips for Advisors." *Advisor Perspectives*, April 8, 2015, https://www.advisorperspectives.com/commentaries/2015/04/08/dalbar-why-investors-suck-and-tips-for-advisors.

46   Neither I nor my publisher has an ownership or commissioned interest in Value Line.

CHAPTER 5:

47   Carla Fried, "Jack Bogle: I Wouldn't Risk Investing Outside the U.S.," *Bloomberg*, December 9, 2014, https://www.bloomberg.com/news/2014-12-08/jack-bogle-i-wouldn-t-risk-investing-outside-the-u-s-.html.

48   Christina Warren, "Facebook Acquires Oculus VR for $2 Billion," *Mashable*, March 25, 2014, http://mashable.com/2014/03/25/facebook-acquires-oculus-vr-for-2-billion/#oFk9wCV6qmq3.

49   Jillian D'Onfro, "Occulus could make up about 10 percent of Facebook's revenue in four years," *Business Insider*, March 31, 2016, http://www.businessinsider.com/analyst-estimates-oculus-revenue-growth-potential-2016-3.

50   Brenna Hillier, "ZeniMax may seek an injunction to halt Oculus Rift sales in wake of broken NDA verdict, details evidence of Oculus's alleged theft," *VG 24/7*, February 2, 2017, http://www.vg247.com/2017/02/02/zenimax-may-seek-an-injunction-to-halt-oculus-rift-sales-in-wake-of-broken-nda-verdict-details-evidence-of-oculuss-alleged-theft/.

51   Andy Patrizio, "Virtual Reality Companies: Top 20 VR Companies to Watch," *Datamation*, April 1, 2016, http://www.datamation.com/mobile-wireless/virtual-reality-companies-top-20-vr-companies-to-watch-1.html.

52   Neither I nor my publisher has any ownership or commissioned interest in HedgeMind.com, but I do use it regularly.

53   Copyright 2017 HedgeMind.com LLC, http://hedgemind.com.

CHAPTER 6:

54   Brad Barber, Yi-Tsung Lee, Yu-Jane Liu, Terrance Odean, "Do Day Traders Rationally Learn About Their Ability?"(academic paper, Berkeley, 2010), https://faculty.haas.berkeley.edu/odean/papers/Day%20Traders/Day%20Trading%20and%20Learning%20110217.pdf.

CHAPTER 7:

55   The Vanguard Group, "Principle 4: Maintain perspective and long-term investing discipline," accessed April 20, 2017, https://personal.vanguard.com/us/insights/investingtruths/investing-truth-about-emotion.

CHAPTER 8:

56   Domini, "Meet Amy Domini," *Domini*, http://domini.com/why-domini/meet-amy-domini.

57   Richard Branson, "Business Needs a Plan B," The Blog, *The Huffington Post*, June 17, 2013, http://www.huffingtonpost.com/richard-branson/business-needs-a-plan-b_b_3456532.html.

58   Bruce Watson, "Natura joins B Corps: will other big business embrace sustainability certification?" *The Guardian*, December 12, 2014, https://www.theguardian.com/sustainable-business/2014/dec/12/b-corps-certification-sustainability-natura.

59   CBS.MarketWatch.com, "Domini 400 Social Index goes live," *MarketWatch*, May 10, 2000, http://www.marketwatch.com/story/domini-400-social-index-goes-live.

60   Financial Advisor, "Socially Responsible Fund Manager Fined For Investing In Sin Companies," *Financial Advisor*, July 30, 2008, http://www.fa-mag.com/news/article-3380.html.

CHAPTER 9:

61   www.reddit.com/r/financialindependence.

62   https://ournextlife.com/ten-questions-to-retire-early/.

Index

Q

Qualified dividends, 82

R

Real estate investing, 13–14, 79–81, 87
Real estate investment trust (REIT), 79–81, 109
Realized capital gain, 5, 82
Rebalancing a portfolio, 50, 96–97, 102
Redemption fee, 72
Registered Investment Advisor (RIA), 45
Research in Motion (RIM), 2
Retirement planning, 14, 57–58, 62–63, 77, 82–84, 97, 157–161
Return on investment, 59–61
Reverse stock split, 37
Risks of not investing, 6–9
Robo-advisors
    description of, 43–44, 49–51
    human advisor *versus*, 53*f*
Rule of 72, 58–59, 58*f*, 63
Russell Indexes, 41, 52, 91

S

S&P 500, 24, 39, 41, 59, 68, 91, 152
S&P bond rating scales, 21*f*
S&P Dow Jones Indices, 39
Saddle strategy, 134
Savings accounts, 7, 14, 76–77, 116, 160
Scottrade, 48
Screening services for socially responsible investing, 151
SEC yield, 70–71
Secondary market, 19
Sector funds, 73
Securities, 7
Securities Act of 1933, 102–103
Securities and Exchange Commission (SEC), 26, 45, 70–75, 74*f*, 78, 135, 137, 137*f*, 154
Selling stocks, 30–36
Settlement date, 31*f*, 32
Shares of stock, 4–5, 5*f*, 36–37
Short position, 136
Short selling, 78, 136
Short-term capital gain, 82, 134
Siegel, Jeremy *(Stocks for the Long Run)*, 89–90, 93
Siemens, 152
Slippage costs, 129–130
Small-cap stocks, 25, 27, 41, 64–66, 65*f*
Snapchat, 86
SnowFinancialGroup.com, 47
Social media for stock apps, 55
Socially responsible investing, 11, 149–156
Soros, George, 124
South Sea Company, 87–88
SPDR S&P 500 Fossil Fuel Free ETF, 156
Spot market, 138
Stock market indexes, 38–41
Stock screeners, 91–92
Stock splits, 36–37

Stock tables, 22–24, 24*f*
Stock tickers, 22–24, 23*f*
Stock(s)
    as currency of a corporation, 3–6
    bonds *versus*, 21–22, 22*f*, 63–64
    buying, 30–36
    class A and B, 16
    common, 15–16
    large-cap, 25
    micro-cap, 26
    mid-cap, 25
    nano-cap, 26
    penny, 26–27, 33, 136–137
    preferred (*See* Preferred stock)
    selection process, 90–100, 121–125
    selling, 30–36
    shares, 4–5
    small-cap, 25, 27
Stop price, 35–36
Stop-limit order, 36
Stop-loss order, 35–36, 112, 125–126
Strangle strategy, 134
Suitability standard of responsibility, 46

T

Target date funds, 77
Tax-loss harvesting, 50
Taxes, 81–84
    as market force, 94
    in options trading, 134
TD Ameritrade, 48, 50
Technical analysis, 102–103
Templeton, Sir John, 89, 91, 95
Term, in bond maturity, 16
Tickers, stock, 22–24, 23*f*
Ticket charge, 30–31
Timing the market, 95–96, 100, 125, 142–143
Timothy Plan, The, 155
TopTenReviews.com, 48
Traders, investors *versus*, 100–101, 101*f*, 129
Trading, 30–36
Trading apps, 54–55
Trading symbols, 23, 70
Trading volume, 26–27
Trailing P/E (price-earnings ratio), 29
Transaction record, 31*f*
Treasury securities, 16–20, 17*f*, 95
Trends, market, 144–146
Trump, Donald, 19

U

Unrealized capital gain, 5
US Treasury, 16, 18
US Treasury securities, 16–20

Notes

REMEMBER TO DOWNLOAD
YOUR FREE DIGITAL ASSETS!

Visit the URL below to access your free Digital Asset files that are included with the purchase of this book.

☑ **Summaries**   ☑ **White Papers**

☑ **Cheat Sheets**   ☑ **Charts & Graphs**

☑ **Articles**   ☑ **Reference Materials**

DOWNLOAD YOURS HERE:

www.clydebankmedia.com/investing-assets

DOWNLOAD A FREE AUDIOBOOK

Explore the World of
FINANCE

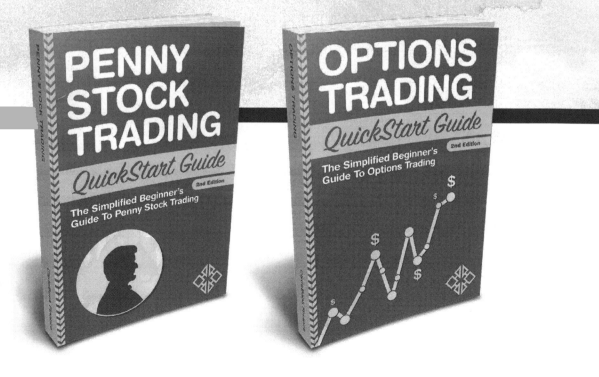

ClydeBank Media is a Proud Sponsor of

AdoptAClassroom.org

AdoptAClassroom.org empowers teachers by providing the classroom supplies and materials needed to help their students learn and succeed. As an award-winning 501(c)(3), AdoptAClassroom.org makes it easy for individual donors and corporate sponsors to donate funds to K-12 classrooms in public, private and charter schools throughout the U.S.

On average, teachers spend $600 of their own money each year to equip their classrooms – 20% of teachers spend more than $1000 annually. Since 1998 AdoptAClassroom.org has raised more than $30 million and benefited more than 4.25 million students. AdoptAClassroom.org holds a 4-star rating from Charity Navigator.

TO LEARN MORE, VISIT ADOPTACLASSROOM.ORG

Made in the USA
Middletown, DE
17 July 2020